WRITERS FOR THE SEVENTIES

Hermann Hesse

WRITERS FOR THE SEVENTIES

Kurt Vonnegut, Jr. by Peter J. Reed

Hermann Hesse by Edwin F. Casebeer

J.R.R. Tolkien by Robley Evans

General Editor: Terence Malley,
Long Island University

HERMANN HESSE

by

Edwin F. Casebeer,

Purdue University (Indianapolis)

THOMAS Y. CROWELL COMPANY
Established 1834
New York 10019

L. C. Card 75-24872

ISBN 0-699-01050-8
    0-690-01051-6 (pbk.)

ACKNOWLEDGMENTS

Reprinted with the permission of Farrar, Straus & Giroux, Inc., from the following titles by Hermann Hesse: NARCISSUS AND GOLDMUND, translated by Ursule Molinaro, copyright © 1968 by Farrar, Straus & Giroux, Inc. From IF THE WAR GOES ON . . . translated by Ralph Manheim, translation copyright © 1970, 1971 by Farrar, Straus & Giroux, Inc.

Hermann Hesse, SIDDHARTHA, translated by Hilda Rosner. Copyright 1951 by New Directions Publishing Corporation. Reprinted by permission of New Directions Publishing Corporation.

From STEPPENWOLF by Hermann Hesse. Translated by Basil Creighton. Copyright 1929 © 1957 by Holt, Rinehart and Winston, Inc. Reprinted by permission of Holt, Rinehart and Winston, Inc.

From THE GLASS BEAD GAME [MAGISTER LUDI] by Hermann Hesse. Translated by Richard and Clara Winston. Copyright © 1969 by Holt, Rinehart and Winston, Inc. Reprinted by permission of Holt, Rinehart and Winston, Inc.

University of North Carolina Studies in the Germanic Languages and Literatures, from HERMANN HESSE AND HIS CRITICS: THE CRITICISM AND BIBLIOGRAPHY OF HALF A CENTURY, by Joseph Mileck (University of North Carolina Studies in the Germanic Languages and Literatures, Vol. 21).

Princeton University Press, from THE COLLECTED WORKS OF C. G. JUNG, edited by G. Adler, M. Fordham, and H. Read, translated by R. F. C. Hull (Bollingen Series XX, Vol. 11: *Psychology and Religion: West and East*). Copyright © 1958 and 1969 by Bollingen Foundation.

My Son
John
This Way

FOREWORD

Hermann Hesse: A Writer for the Seventies

Hermann Hesse, by Edwin F. Casebeer, is one volume in a series of critical appreciations under the collective title, "Writers for the Seventies." Other books in this series are *Kurt Vonnegut, Jr.,* by Peter J. Reed; *J.R.R. Tolkien,* by Robley Evans; and *Richard Brautigan,* by Terence Malley. The intention of these studies is to provide clear and balanced discussions of the main themes and techniques of the four authors in question. In each case, the critic has tried to avoid excessively technical, academic terminology. In general—though of course this will vary

11

from book to book—the four critics have addressed their subjects directly or even personally, without the sort of detachment that makes so many critical studies seem remote. Hopefully, the volumes in the Writers for the Seventies series will serve as good introductions to the four authors under discussion, for readers only slightly familiar with their books, while offering fresh insights for those who have already read the major works of Hesse, Tolkien, Vonnegut, and Brautigan.

A second—less direct—intention of the Writers for the Seventies series is to help, in a small way, to bridge that large and apparently increasing gap between the high school and college age readers of today and their parents and/or teachers. The four critics involved in this project are all youngish professors at various American colleges. All four are in their thirties: old enough to have their graduate training in what seems already, only ten or twelve years later, a time of relatively settled, traditional standards; young enough to feel the impact of today's counter-culture and to be aware of their students' insistence on "relevance" in literature. In each volume, the emphasis is on critical *appreciation;* in each case, the critic tries to arrive at qualitative judgments about his author's achievement and to define the value of this author for readers of all ages.

But why these four authors in particular? Why Hesse, Tolkien, Vonnegut, and Brautigan? Early in his book, *Future Shock,* Alvin Toffler asserts that "Writers have a harder and harder time keeping up with reality."* And, of course, it is possible that the "reality" captured by these four writers will soon cease to hold the attention of readers, that each of the four will soon be seen as someone who had a certain vogue in the late 1960s and early 1970s and then faded off the bookstore racks and out of the mind of readers. This is possible, but not, I think, probable. Despite the vagaries of taste and popularity, the strange chemistry that makes today's best seller next

---

*New York: Bantam Books, 1971, p. 5.

year's remainder item, it seems likely that all four authors focused upon in the Writers for the Seventies series will continue to hold the attention of American readers, particularly younger readers of high school and college ages.

Needless to say, the four authors are very different: Hesse, the pacifist, deep in Eastern religions and Jungian psychology; Tolkien, the Oxford don, absorbed in medieval literature and philology; Vonnegut, the former PR man turned satirist of an increasingly dehumanized America; Brautigan, that transitional figure between the Beat Generation and the Hippies, concerned with a gentle world of trout fishing and green growing things. Indeed, if we were to imagine the four of them in some Paradise of Authors (or—that favorite test-question situation—cast up together on a desert island), we might very well decide that they would have little to say to each other, about their works, about their interests.

Yet for all their differences, there are some important common denominators running through the works of Hesse, Tolkien, Vonnegut, and Brautigan. Perhaps outlining a few of them will partly explain why all four writers began to attract large audiences in the United States at approximately the same time. First of all, speaking broadly, all four can be described as fantasy-writers. Whether through interior fantasies (like *Steppenwolf* and *In Watermelon Sugar*) or through exterior fantasies (like *The Lord of the Rings* and *The Sirens of Titan*)— all four authors use fantasy to comment on reality. Of course, any successful fantasy (from fairy tale to science fiction) comments in some way or other on ordinary reality. But our four authors have all, in their very different ways, been able to give their fantasies the sort of internal coherence, plausibility, and substance that enable their readers to suspend disbelief and accept what Coleridge called the "poetic truth" behind fantasy.

In common with virtually every significant writer of the last half-century, the reality behind their fantasies is pretty grim. In all four authors, a war—World War I or World War II—serves as either implicit or explicit background. The appalling catastrophe of the First World War, the slaughter of an entire generation of young men, seems always just beneath the surface of Hesse's major works; in Tolkien, the vast carnage of World War II paralleled exactly the composition of his own version of an ultimate struggle between forces of light and darkness; the Second World War has had the most direct influence on Vonnegut, who was in the war, a POW and a miraculous survivor of the hideous fire-bombing of Dresden; for Brautigan, the youngest of the four authors, World War II is coincident with his earliest conscious memories, and stands ironically as a time of coherence, when things were easier to understand than they could ever be again.

All four authors would surely agree with the "moral" of Vonnegut's *Mother Night:* "We are what we pretend to be, so we must be careful about what we pretend to be." In all four, this bare statement is developed in rich, complex terms. All four are ultimately concerned with self-definition, with the problem of a person's realizing his full humanity (or, in Tolkien's case, I suppose we must also say his full hobbithood). In all four, self-fulfillment is threatened by an essentially dehumanized and dehumanizing world: Hesse's world of vulgar materialism, Tolkien's world in which Sauron aspires to enslave the spirits of all living creatures, Vonnegut's world in which machines often threaten to replace humanity, Brautigan's world of dropouts from a society without sustaining values.

Finally—and perhaps the most important thing Hesse, Tolkien, Vonnegut, and Brautigan have in common—all four authors share an affirmative sense of the possibilities of the human spirit. Without denying the pitfalls that surround their characters, without settling for facile optimism, all four of these Writers for the Seventies show us in their works that there are still things a person can do, that there are still values to be found by looking around oneself and (even more important) by looking *within* oneself. In this time of disillusionment and danger,

14

we need writers like Hesse, Tolkien, Vonnegut, and Brautigan—to remind us that joy is still possible, to teach us (in Hesse's phrase) how to hear the laughter of the immortals.

Although he makes reference to various other works, in *Hermann Hesse* Edwin F. Casebeer concentrates on the four major novels written by Hesse between 1922 and 1943: *Siddhartha, Steppenwolf, Narcissus and Goldmund, Magister Ludi (The Glass Bead Game)*. The time-span is obviously significant; the earliest of the four, *Siddhartha*, was written from among the ruins of the First World War (and, coincidentally, from among the ruins of Hesse's own personal life), while the latest, *Magister Ludi*, was completed as the wreckage of a second and even more devastating world war continued to mount. As much as any of his contemporaries—as much as Spengler or Yeats, as much as Pound or Eliot—Hesse was aware of the prevalent physical, intellectual, moral, and spiritual exhaustion of his time, of this age which he calls in *Magister Ludi* "the Century of Wars."

Yet for Hesse, this painful sense of "an age that has lost its bearings" was a starting point rather than a conclusion. Throughout his major works, Hesse leads his readers, as well as his characters, on journeys of discovery. These journeys may be literal (like the vagabondage of Goldmund, in *Narcissus and Goldmund*) or they may be interior (like Harry Haller's strange progress through the fantastic Magic Theater, in *Steppenwolf*); they are always journeys toward self-knowledge. The knowledge that is to be gained—and, paradoxically, the knowledge that is to be *taught* through Hesse's books—always transcends book-learning. The final wisdom is always to be gained through living.

The wisdom toward which Hesse can start us on our own journeys is nothing less than a sense of the real priorities of life. "Learn what is to be taken seriously," says Pablo to Harry Haller, near the end of *Steppenwolf*,

15

"and laugh at the rest." Obviously, this sense of life's priorities is one of the hardest things to learn. The journey requires intelligence, imagination—and courage.

Reading Edwin Casebeer's discussions of Hesse's novels, we inevitably feel his own deep involvement in Hesse's works. For, as Casebeer says, the only way to really read Hesse is to participate in the books, even as Hesse participated by making his protagonists projections of aspects of his own personality. The journeys in these novels do not pertain only to Siddhartha or Harry Haller or Joseph Knecht; they are our journeys too.

The goal of each of these journeys into oneself is the "cheerful serenity" that characterizes the succession of figures in Hesse's novels which Casebeer refers to as "Old Men"—men beyond the bewildering dualities, apparent chaos, and seeming evils of life. Men who have reached what Hesse calls, in *Narcissus and Goldmund,* an "agreement with life."

Terence Malley
Long Island University
Brooklyn, New York

TABLE OF CONTENTS

PREFACE

In 1958, Joseph Mileck, one of the most conscientious American scholars of Hermann Hesse, concluded his survey of Western criticism of the novelist:

> Immersed as he is in the romantic tradition of Novalis, a tradition which is neither understood nor appreciated by the American, Hesse is not likely to attract many readers here except for a few kindred spirits in our university circles, and for the German speaking intellectuals who have

emigrated to America in the past two decades. Hesse is himself convinced that America will never prove receptive to his works.[1]

Both Mileck and Hesse were dramatically wrong. The New Directions paperback edition of *Siddhartha* (1957) has had nineteen printings. Between 1968 and 1969, Farrar ran nine printings of *Narcissus and Goldmund;* there were plans to print 400,000 paperbacks.

Obviously, the America that Hesse was so dubious about is going through a remarkable change—at least among the young men and women who are spiritually in tune with the "counter culture." Why? I can give two answers, which will provide the theme for my book. First, Hesse believed that the universe makes sense; we need such affirmation today. Second, Hesse believed that the best way to realize that affirmation is to realize yourself. It is that obligation that brings the young again and again into conflict with their more conforming elders and rulers. Self-realization requires great freedom and great tolerance of differences. It requires the patience to see trial after trial become error after error, and the courage to recognize that complete success will come to the individual only when it has come to the species. In a world that complicates their difficult journey by its fear of their example, the young need assurance and guidance through the hazards of creating a new culture counter to our conformist, organized, mechanical technocracy so stifling to the new individualism that it, ironically, gave the environment to develop. By his novels and by his life (they unite), Hermann Hesse gives them the assurance and guidance of a man who sought himself through eighty five years of the most disastrous events of our age.

My book contains chapters on four of Hesse's novels most popular in the counter culture: *Siddhartha, Steppenwolf, Narcissus and Goldmund,* and *Magister Ludi (The Glass Bead Game).* Together these novels show an amazing breadth of subjects, situations, characters, themes, and techniques. Yet underlying them all is a unifying theme: the search for self-realization in a harmonious universe.

My decision to omit consideration of *Demian,* surely one of Hesse's most popular novels, requires some explanation. When I first read *Demian* it had great impact on me. But the impact wasn't from Sinclair or Demian or Mother Eva. It was from the strange and reassuring things Hesse *said* when he stopped writing the novel and spoke about his beliefs; I virtually memorized the Preface and the passages on the god-devil Abraxas and Pistorius' lecture on the air bladder. I was compelled and strengthened by the command to immerse myself in the horror of my life. But there were problems. As a novel, *Demian* seemed to me to be ruptured. Up through *Demian* Hesse's fiction took the conventional German form of the *Bildungsroman* (the novel of personal development); in effect, his novels were often thinly disguised autobiographies. But the traumas of World War I, his wife's insanity, their divorce, his own breakdown, and especially, his subsequent psychoanalysis by a Jungian gave Hesse insights that he could no longer contain in the *Bildungsroman,* insights that split *Demian* apart. Hesse was driven to other forms of expression: the legend of *Siddhartha,* the surrealism of *Steppenwolf,* the historical romance of *Narcissus and Goldmund,* the collage of essay-biography-poetry-tale of *Magister Ludi.* These novels are ultimately as intimate as any of the early novels but their form objectifies them, univeralizes them, and makes them into open-ended experiences that others can enter with greater ease. I can't enter *Demian* easily; Sinclair doesn't move me and Demian moves me too much. I think that Demian is the most dangerous of Hesse's heroes to use as a model; it would require the wisdom of a Joseph Knecht, the Magister Ludi, to contain the power of a Demian. I think Hesse regarded Demian as a problem rather than a solution: he didn't really begin to cope with Demian until *Steppenwolf* and didn't come to terms with him until *Narcissus and Goldmund.*

A word about the organization of this book. In each chapter, I emphasize a particular problem and adopt a particular approach. I make a standard analysis of plot, character, tone, and theme in *Siddhartha;* the specific problem I emphasize is that posed by the use of oriental mysticism in the novel. The "Magic Theater" of *Steppenwolf* introduces another approach, the analysis of dream structure; the new subject is Jung's theory of the personality—its ego, anima, and Self. *Narcissus and Goldmund* takes me deeper into Jungianism, into the archetypes of the primal mother and father; the emphasis now is on the symbolic imagery. *Magister Ludi* takes me into the aesthetics of music and the Glass Bead Game; here I use no specific analytical approach but draw on the others where it is useful to do so.

I would like to close this Preface with some warnings. The chapters are progressively difficult and should be read in order. The subjects and approaches that I have centered on in each novel are not unique to that novel—they pervade all four novels. My use of orientalism, Jungianism, and aesthetics is strictly amateur; I explored these areas just enough to open up Hesse and then I let him take over. My strength, such as it is, is in literature—and English literature, not German. In places—in my discussion of *Siddhartha's* symbol of the stone, for instance, or in my remarks about Hermine and about Goldmund's mother-world and death—I will be struggling with questions rather than providing slick, easy answers. I'm a person who has liked Hesse for some fifteen years, trying to communicate the pleasures and profundities I have found in his work. Learn from my failures by understanding *why* I failed. Above all, listen to yourself—along with me and, more important, along with Hesse. It is his major lesson and the hardest of all to learn. Hesse tells us, "We can understand one another; but each of us is able to interpret himself to himself alone."[2]

CHAPTER ONE

Siddhartha: The Completed Hero

Brought out as a New Directions Paperback in 1957,[1] *Siddhartha* is very likely the most popular of Hesse's books. When I first began to read Hesse in 1958, it was particularly popular among those college students attracted to the figures of San Francisco's North Beach "beat" movement (Ferlinghetti was also being published by New Directions, a company making available to the country the best and most remarkable books produced by the American avant-garde or by previously untranslated foreign authors). At its earliest development, that Pacific

Coast movement—virtually the midwife of today's youth counter culture—was deeply concerned with Oriental mysticism; Alan Watts' *The Way of Zen* was an equal favorite. With the well-known avant-garde publisher behind it and a clear American interest in its subject matter, *Siddhartha* had the proper beginnings for the popularity it has since attained: nineteen paperback printings over the past thirteen years. *Magister Ludi* and the Nobel Prize may have secured Hesse's reputation among English-speaking intelligentsia by 1946, but I doubt that such an event was as important to his present reputation as was New Directions' decision to have Hilda Rosner translate *Siddhartha* in 1951 and then to bring out the novella in a low-cost paperback in 1957. *Siddhartha* is so brief, so simple, and—as I will demonstrate—so central to the world of the other major Hesse novels that it provides the quickest and most thorough initial experience of Hesse with the least expenditure of time.

Putting aside the circumstances of its introduction to the American public and its simplicity, why did *Siddhartha* become so important in those days? To me, and I imagine to others of my generation (the silent one) who were reading it in the late '50's, it was one of the few affirmations being made in a society dominated by pessimism and hyperrationalism: The universe was absurd, man and society were fragmented, institutions were empty of relevant content. The only demonstrable facts were that each of us is isolated from the other and that all of us are subject to death, facts that rendered meaningless all that we did, individually or collectively. Although the resultant responses to these "facts" ranged widely from suicidal nihilism to heroic efforts to erect foundations in the quicksand, few disagreed with the basic pessimistic propositions. Thus, by its elders, was the problem defined for the silent generation. But where were the solutions?

Hesse offered one. For him, the universe hung together. It was harmonious. It included man. It was folly to focus upon the ego, to consider oneself a discrete individual.

Certainly, the individual is isolated in some very important and fundamental ways even from the individual closest to him. Certainly, the individual will die. But to Hesse the most important fact about each of us was not our individuality but our relationship to the whole universe. Siddhartha elaborates upon the point with the metaphor of the stone. First, he thought the stone was simply a stone. He realized, however, that within the continual change of mass to energy and back again, the stone could become other things. Finally, he realized that "it has already long been everything and always is everything." In other words, the stone has the potential of everything it has been or participated within in the past—plant, animal, man—and it has the potential of everything that it will be or participated within in the future; given an infinity of time, it has the potential of becoming everything in the universe. Finally, if the distinction between *been, being,* and *becoming* is artificial and arbitrary, the stone is *now* everything it has been and everything it potentially will be. And so is man, as is Siddhartha himself when Govinda kisses his brow and sees thousands of selves, man and animal, flow beneath that face which has now become like the surface of the river from which Siddhartha learned so much. And yet, Siddhartha points out, the stone *is* a stone, individual and unique and quite concrete as well as a universe of possibilities. And, in that sense, each of our egos does exist. Neither they nor the death, isolation, and pain they suffer are illusory. But these defeats are only part of reality. Beyond our egos is the universe to which they belong, with which they will merge, from which they will re-emerge. We are not limited to a single role, trapped within a single personality—not even during our one physical life (Siddhartha becomes *six* men). We must recognize that we are *already* that which we strive to be, that the *future,* as well as the past, is in the present, that *eternity is now.*[2]

These were powerful words of encouragement in the 1950's. They were also obscure, paradoxical, elusive words. Even Siddhartha said that words inadequately expressed the happy world view that he held. But the happiness of it, the calm certainty in the tone of Hesse's novella, the wide range of allusions to the Orient, to another culture which might have solutions to the entrapment of Western man in death and despair—these were enough to make the book very attractive then and, I imagine, now. Simply, it opened doors. One might turn from it to Vedanta, Buddhism, Yoga, Taoism, to such contemporary intellectuals as Alan Watts, who, like Hesse, was attempting to give modern man a basis for hope and optimism by synthesizing Eastern thought with Western psychotherapy. Such a synthesis, though still barely begun, has gained tremendous momentum recently in the youth culture, resulting in deep and widespread interest in the *Bhagavad-Gita* and *Upanishads*, the *Tao Te Ching* and the *I Ching*, Zen Buddhism, the Maharishi Mahesh Yogi's Students' International Meditation Society (SIMS), Hatha Yoga, Meher Baba, Gurdjieff and the Sufi system. If the absorption in the Orient should evolve from fad to cultural fact, it easily could develop a change in the quality of Western life equal to that initiated by the Arabs when they reintroduced the West to Greek knowledge and provided the groundwork for the Renaissance.

On the other hand, it is just that quality of *Siddhartha* which I have been discussing so favorably that is likely to put off another group of readers which might be drawn to the book otherwise: the terminology of Vedanta and Buddhism, *Brahmin, Brahman, Atman, Om, Prajapati, Satya, Samana, Nirvana, Gotama,* the Four Main Points and the Eightfold Path, *Mara, Maya, Samsara,* and the references to the *Upanishads* and *Vedas*, the *Upanishads of Sama-Veda, Chandogya Upanishads, Rig-Veda, Yoga-Veda, Arthava-Veda.*

Although it would seem that Hesse here requires a prolonged prefatory course of Oriental studies as prerequisite to the understanding of his novella, such, I believe, is not the case. In fact, he observed that he himself was rather rusty in an area once his major interest and that, after writing the beginning of *Siddhartha* in which most of the terminology appears, he had

> to recollect and deepen my memories of the life of asceticism and meditation before I could once again find my way in the world of the Indian spirit that I had found holy and congenial since early youth.[3]

In actuality, terminology need not be a major block to the appreciation and understanding of the main features of the novella. First, there are not too many such references: I have listed most of them and a casual inspection of *Siddhartha* will reveal that the bulk of these words appear in Part One, the first quarter of the book. Second, I would stress that Siddhartha *rejects* the teachings of both Brahminism and Buddhism, a fact which accounts not only for the limitation of most of the terminology to the first quarter of the book where this rejection occurs, but also supports the notion that Hesse feels that the way to Siddhartha's spiritual perfection is much simpler. In fact, the reader could regard his sense of the vast and intricate complexities that such terminology evokes as being quite necessary to the success of this phase of the novella: Siddhartha, too, is puzzled, blocked by learning and teachers and the stress on information and knowledge. The uninitiated reader shares in Siddhartha's confusion (while some of the initiate have expressed to me their provocation with some of Hesse's inaccuracies, e.g., the fictional *Yoga-Veda*).

Nevertheless, a little knowledge (very basic and very oversimplified) of Brahminism might render comfort and security as well as stress those aspects of the religion which Hesse knows and esteems and with which he certainly agrees. *Siddhartha* takes place at a crucial point in Indian history, about five hundred years before Christ when Gotama Buddha is winning disciples to his religion. Siddhartha belongs to the Hindu upper classes, to the Brahmin or priest class, which was sometimes in

Indian history considered higher than that of kings or princes; the lower classes would treat Siddhartha with considerable respect. Had he lived his life normally, he would have been first a student of the *Vedas*, the scriptures of his religion. Then, like his father, he would marry, sire children, and maintain a household. Third, he would become a religious hermit. He would end his life as a holy beggar.

At the opening of the book, Siddhartha is in the first phase: He is a student, a role which requires listening to lectures and engaging in debate upon his religion. Central to that religion are the *Vedas* which he quotes from occasionally. The *Vedas* (the word means "knowledge") are roughly equivalent to our Bible, offering over a hundred books of legend, philosophy, poetry. A special feature of the *Vedas* is their *mantras* or hymns, the oldest and most cherished collection being in the *Rig-Veda*. The *Upanishads* are the last sections of the four *Vedas: Rig-Veda, Sama-Veda, Yajur-Veda,* and *Atharva-Veda.* They are somewhat mystical, somewhat philosophical in nature; they have been abstracted and condensed in the *Bhagavad-Gita.* The *Upanishads* provide the doctrine for the *Vedanta Sutras,* from which in turn most of Hindu thought has evolved. Central among the *Upanishads'* doctrine and important to this novella is the equation of Atman (the Self) with Brahman (the Universe), a point which I shall develop shortly. After his rejection of the Samanas, Siddhartha gives up *Atharva-Veda* and *Yoga-Veda.* Since the *Artharva-Veda* is a popular collection of spells, curses, etc., and since some practitioners of Yoga (a "Yoga-Veda" does not exist) come to stress magical powers over nature, Hesse is underlining the Samanas' apparent emphasis on magic rather than on obtaining *Nirvana,* a much nobler goal.

Some clarification of what is meant by "meditation" as Siddhartha practices it among the Brahmins and the Samanas would help the reader to understand the peculiar character of Siddhartha's psychological state, which Hesse tries to evoke by tone, atmosphere and—

28

in the German—the language.[4] "Meditation" is a term to be understood as it is used in the United States presently by adherents of such groups as the Maharishi's Students' International Meditation Society (SIMS). Siddhartha breathes in a specific pattern and repeats to himself a *mantra* or religious incantation, the purpose of which is to induce in him a form of concentration uncommon to Westerners: he seeks a state in which he no longer reasons, remembers, analyzes or performs any other intellectual function upon objects as if they were external to himself; he and the objects "outside" become one as the mental state becomes a pure awareness of and identification with the universe in a mood of absolute peace and tranquillity. Some SIMS members of my acquaintance refer to the experience as "tripping out"— the state not only has some relationship to the psychedelic experience (which will be encountered, by the way, in *Steppenwolf's* Magic Theater) in its quality but also seems to have some physiological connection in that psychedelic drugs interfere with its occurrence.

The syllable *Om* which Siddhartha apparently uses as a *mantra* (it begins and ends all Brahmin prayers) is important to this novella, for it is the syllable that the river utters at a crucial moment in the conclusion. Its three letters (actually, A-U-M) stand for the three most important *Vedas;* the three elements of the universe; the three gods Brahma, Vishnu, and Siva, and so on—in short, as a friend of mine has remarked, "*Om* summarizes all of Hinduism." The stress that Hesse places on the syllable concerns this *unifying* or summarizing power. Thus in the chapter "Om" Siddhartha, after hearing in the sound of the river every possible voice, finally perceives that they all blend together: "the great song of a thousand voices consisted of one word: Om—perfection" (p. 111).

This sense of unity is also stressed by Hesse in his frequent references to *Atman* and *Brahman*. In its simplest terms, Hesse's major point in this novella is that the individual human being and the universe are *one* thing, not two things. In Part One, Siddhartha is largely concerned

29

with either stifling or finding out about *Atman* or the subjective and particular self called "Siddhartha." Among the Samanas, he tries to deny this Self to find *Brahma*, which seems to him to be all the objective world that exists outside him and from which he feels vitally isolated. He is, of course, mistaken. *Brahma* includes him and always has. *Brahma* is in reality the central principle of the universe—the creative principle—the force that lies in all things (including Siddhartha) and unites them in one harmonious universe which is of *a single piece*. Thus, the ultimate reality is that the subjective and the objective worlds are one: *Brahma-Atman*.[5] Upon entering awareness of this unity of *Brahma* and *Atman*, the Brahmin or Samana simultaneously enter the indescribably exhilarating state which they—and Siddhartha—covet so much: *Nirvana*.

The above should suffice as a general introduction.[6] I will let *Siddhartha* itself make further distinctions.

The plot of *Siddhartha* is easy to summarize. In search of universal truth, Siddhartha, a young Indian Brahmin, together with his friend Govinda, abandons the community and religious practices of his parents to become a wandering ascetic beggar, a Samana. The two in turn leave the Samanas to hear Gotama Buddha, who is winning converts to his religion; while Govinda is impressed by Buddha and becomes a disciple, Siddhartha concludes that nothing is to be learned from teachers and decides to turn to the world of the common man to find his answers.

There Kamala, the prostitute, instructs him thoroughly in eroticism (the whole of the *Kama Sutra*!) and introduces him to the rich merchant Kamaswami, under whom Siddhartha becomes a successful and wealthy man due to his ability to transform his religious theory and discipline into business practice. But this life also becomes unsatisfactory; Siddhartha not only feels himself becoming stunted but remains isolated from these "Kamaswami people"—he is aloof, unable to love. Nauseated by his life and his new addiction to gambling, Siddhartha leaves his home and Kamala, who unknown to him is to have his child.

Siddhartha finally reaches his goal while working with Vasudeva, a simple ferryman, beside a river. He goes through two phases: first, after long suffering of un-requited love for his newly discovered son, the aristo-cratic Siddhartha is finally humbled enough to identify with the rest of mankind; second, after gaining wisdom in his association with Vasudeva and the river, Siddhartha transcends his troublesome Self and becomes one with the universe. When his friend Govinda comes upon him at the end of the book, Siddhartha has gained the stature of a god.

Such a book is best approached by those who seek calm. It is written in a low key. The plot does have mo-ments of drama: Siddhartha's confrontation with his father; his conquering of the Samana; his "awakening" after he leaves Buddha and Govinda; his near-suicide after he leaves Kamala and Kamaswami; and his anguished love for his son. Yet the tone in which these incidents are presented and the emotional texture of those incidents which surround them, the rhythmic na-ture of the sentences and the plot-delaying passages of imagery, all unite to present the reader an experience which leads to tranquillity. The events and people are far away in space and in time as are the events and people of legends. There is little sense of conflict between the hero and those about him. There is even little such sense of conflict within him—such a prominent feature of *Steppenwolf* and *Narcissus and Goldmund.*

Instead of conflict, the moving force of *Siddhartha*'s plot is that of the search for Self. As Hesse observes in the "Treatise of the Steppenwolf":

> The heroes of the epics of India are not individ-uals, but whole reels of individualities in a series of incarnations.[7]

31

This is very much like the movement of *Siddhartha*'s plot. The first "individual of the reel" is the scholarly son of the aristocratic Brahmin, highly accomplished in the theology of the sect and in its disciplines. He does not find satisfaction with Self. Siddhartha the Brahmin ends and a new individual emerges: Siddhartha the Samana. As an ascetic, he now attempts to destroy Self by self-deprivation and meditative techniques which create a selfless empathy with things eternal. Again, he meets defeat. He leaves the search for knowledge through teachers and begins to search for wisdom through experience. And more "reels of individualities" appear.

Siddhartha becomes a sensualist, the lover of one of India's most accomplished courtesans. He becomes a businessman who attains great success and power. But these selves are not *the* Self he has now vowed to discover. Nauseated by this life, Siddhartha leaves it and emerges as a new individual: Siddhartha, helper of the ferryman Vasudeva. Though he has neared his goal, Siddhartha has yet one more self to experience: Siddhartha the father, crucified by unreciprocated love. And this individual also passes.

So far, Siddhartha's selves have rapidly succeeded one another in time: scholar, ascetic, sensualist, businessman, laborer, father. But at the end of his life, in his encounter with Govinda, Siddhartha's life ceases to exist in time. Simultaneously, in one moment and at one point in space, he explodes into all being. Siddhartha's "self" is the universe Govinda sees in him:

> Other faces, many faces, a long series, a continuous stream of faces—hundreds, thousands, which all came and disappeared and yet all seemed to be there at the same time, which all continually changed and renewed themselves and which were yet all Siddhartha (p. 121).

The plot presents Siddhartha living and dying in six distinct selves (two incarnations at each social level on a descending scale) and at the end of the novel integrating those selves with all of the possible selves of the universe, transcending the self defined as that isolated, perishable ego within each of us to become a Self that contains all of us, to become a God, even more than a God—a Universe of All Being.

This lack of conflict can be further explained by observing the divisions of its structure. Although Hesse himself divides *Siddhartha* into two parts, in actuality the book divides into three sections, each four chapters long.[8] In the first, Siddhartha rejects the life of the intellect. In the second, he rejects the life of the senses. In the third, through the suffering of love and the experience of universal reality in the simplest of natural phenomenon, the river, Siddhartha identifies with the universe. Such a structure explains further the lack of exciting conflict. Whereas in *Steppenwolf* the hero is continually and violently torn between his simultaneous commitments to the lives of the intellect and the senses, Siddhartha first explores the province of the intellect and *then* turns to that of the senses. Neither world enters the other, and thus the novel remains comparatively simple emotionally. This three-part structure will form the structure of my chapter until its conclusion. Within the discussion of each part I will pay particular attention to developments in plot, character, and theme for two major purposes: (1) to stress the unique emotional values not so readily apparent in this novel, and (2) to clarify as much as possible Hesse's meaning.

The first section (Chapters One to Four) demonstrates why Siddhartha rejected the life of the intellect. Each of the first three chapters reveals him discarding an intellectual tactic: (1) Brahminism, (2) Samanic asceticism, (3) Buddhism. The fourth chapter powerfully presents the death of Siddhartha the intellectual and his rebirth into a life of the senses. Siddhartha's rejection of Brahminism is first a rejection of family and social class; he realizes early in his youth (the first section concludes before he reaches twenty) that family and friends cannot fulfill him. He searches the religion and philosophy of Brahminism for peace, satisfaction, happiness. The religious ritual is soothing, but other elements, such as the pantheon of gods, are unbelievable. Siddhartha intuits that a single universal being or principle exists and, further, that it lies within his soul. But he does not know what his soul is or the way to enter into it except through sleep or deep meditation; yet once conscious again, he, like the other Brahmins, strives, sins, suffers. Siddhartha wants the heaven of the soul with him every moment. And the Brahmins cannot provide this bliss.

So Siddhartha searches among the Samanas. Rather than living in the comfort of the Brahmins, he now punishes his body by fasting and looks upon the rest of humanity with cold contempt. Rather than searching for peace by searching for his soul, he now attempts to destroy Self, to destroy his personality so that the universal being, the heaven obscured by the self, might be revealed to him. He learns to lose his personality through yoga practices that enable him to unify his being with the beings of things outside him: "animal, carcass, stone, wood, water" (p. 12). But though he can lose the self temporarily, he always awakes to find it still there. Finally, Siddhartha concludes that the flight from self was no more than the temporary anaesthesia that could be obtained in a night of drinking. He concludes further that the truth that he sought can never be found by learning, that the worst barrier to the knowledge that he sought was the teacher.

When Siddhartha and Govinda leave the Samanas, Siddhartha already has arrived at the main insight of the first section. His questioning of the new religion of Buddha emphasizes the futility of learning through the intellect. In his debate with Gotama Buddha, Siddhartha admits that Buddha, among all men, has found what Siddhartha seeks. He has been certain of this fact from the moment that he first saw him and recognized the perfect peace within him and saw that he knew the

Truth. But though he instantly esteemed and even loved the Buddha, he realized that Buddha would be unable to *teach* him how he had become what he was. And he perceived that Buddha is the greatest teacher that humanity has produced.

In Chapter Four, Siddhartha ends the quest through the intellect and turns to the use of his senses to find his goal. His problem now comes more clearly into focus; his main concern has been his self, his sense of being an isolated individual, unrelated to the world about him. He has foolishly attempted to escape the self by denying it in order to reach the desired state of nirvanic bliss, peace, and satisfaction. He realizes that he does not really know his self, for he has spent his life avoiding it, and he vows to begin to explore it:

> I will learn from myself, be my own pupil; I will learn from myself the secret of Siddhartha (p. 32).

In short, Siddhartha has decided to turn from *teaching* to *experience* as a mode of learning. As he will say later in the novella, he comes to seek *wisdom* through *living* rather than *knowledge* through *learning*. Immediately the beauty of the nature which he had rejected as Brahmin and Samana opens up to his senses and he realizes:

> Meaning and reality were not hidden somewhere behind things, they were in them, in all of them (p. 32).

After a moment of powerful despair when he sees how his new viewpoint cuts him off from his entire past, Siddhartha moves on to the next phase of his quest.

When I have summarized thematic development as I have above, it would seem that I have pretty well taken care of Part One. Here, along with the proliferation of Brahmin terminology, we have another problem in Part One which might initially discourage the reader. The

problem is that the presentation of an intellectual existence offers little obvious opportunity for drama. Actual
dramatized incidents having a relatively strong emotional
impact are rare: Siddhartha's confrontations with his
father and with the leader of the Samanas. The other
"dramatized" incidents are largely discussions with Govinda or with Buddha or are internal monologues presenting Siddhartha's evolving philosophy. Siddhartha's life
among the Brahmins and among the Samanas is summarized rather quickly and sketchily. There are relatively
few images to hold onto—the tropical river of the Brahmins; bodily pain and incarnations into animals as a
Samana; the quiet gatherings at Buddha's pleasure
garden and the burst of nature imagery at Siddhartha's
"awakening."

With the exception of Siddhartha himself, the characters are also sketchy. Govinda chiefly functions to give
Hesse an alternative method of presenting Siddhartha's
ideas; he is loyal, loving, passive, simple-minded and
therefore fortunately prone to ask just the right questions.
Siddhartha's father has some strength and individuality:
he is a man who is controlled, calm, and gentle; who is
provoked into a stubborn and uncharacteristically brutal
anger towards his son; and who finally submits to that
son because of his own anxiety, fear, and sorrow. But the
man has barely a page in the novella. The old Samana is
vividly malignant, willful, and rather stupid, but he receives even less space than the father. Buddha sounds as
Buddha reads—his dialogue is a theological treatise.

Yet Siddhartha has character. The incident with his
father reveals in Siddhartha an odd blend of the gentle
and the powerful. His defeat of the Samana displays the
same powerful will now combined with an unusual occult
talent that prefigures his future achievements. The conversations with Govinda and Buddha reveal a young man
totally committed to the mind and expert enough in its
control to debate with the greatest intellectual of his age.

Siddhartha's internal monologues are most interesting
to me, especially the one which dominates the fourth

and last chapter of this section. The earlier monologues present clearly his initial dissatisfaction, his many questions, his thirst for ultimate knowledge; his growing aloofness among the Samanas, his single-minded asceticism, his growing scepticism and delicately ironic humor, his extraordinary self-possession before the eldest Samana; his initial timidity, developing self-confidence and poise, and final awe before Buddha.

But the last monologue, the dramatization of Siddhartha's "awakening," has the most dramatic interest, not only among the internal monologues but also among the dialogues and incidents that have taken place up to this point. With its companion end-chapters Eight and Twelve, it supports strongly the contention that the most compelling aspect of *Siddhartha* is its spiritual drama. Chapter Four begins in reflection, deepening into the mystic's meditation which produces two intellectual insights which freeze him in his progress out of Buddha's pleasure garden. The awakening begins with a smile, a quickened pace, and a strong sense of euphoria in response to the lush nature of which he is suddenly aware. The euphoria culminates in an exhilarating sense of rebirth or "awakening," undercut suddenly by his realization that he is isolated, that all has ended. The insight produces in him "an icy chill"—he "shivered inwardly like a small animal" (p. 33). His isolation from Govinda, from his father and family, even from the Samanas is a terrible fact widening and deepening his despair. But he continues to pursue his destiny:

> At that moment, when the world around him melted away, when he stood alone like a star in the heavens, he was overwhelmed by a feeling of icy despair, but he was more firmly himself than ever. That was the last shudder of his awakening, the last pains of birth (p. 34).

Of the three sections, the second presents the fewest emotional or intellectual problems, for Siddhartha is in "our world," the world of whores and businessmen. Such unfamiliarity as there is develops within Siddhartha, not within us, as he confronts what is to him a totally alien experience. His very surprise and naiveté allow us nearer to him as a character than did his previous spiritual intellectuality; even his subsequent unappealing callousness and his nauseated despair are more familiar. However, though the texture of Siddhartha's experience has a customary feel to it, we should not be disarmed: Siddhartha rejects "our world." The basis for that rejection must be made clear, for that is the point of this section.

The second section of *Siddhartha* certainly contains much more variety and many more episodes than the first. Although the sense of narrative complexity is partially illusory in that many of these incidents are simply and briefly summarized, those which Hesse goes to the trouble of working up dramatically through the development of imagery and dialogue are frequent enough, possess much more "human" substance, and contain the major plot developments of this section: Siddhartha's ecstatic sensual response to nature; the odd erotic dream of Govinda as bisexual; the pleasant encounter with Vasudeva; the highly erotic one with the peasant girl; the detailed development of the meeting of Siddhartha and Kamala; the interview with Kamaswami; Kamaswami's bewilderment at Siddhartha's lack of avarice; the peaking of his love affair with Kamala; the deepest stage of self-disgust with his materially successful life and his departure from the pleasure garden; and the extremely powerful final chapter of the second section ("By the River"), which brings Siddhartha to the point of suicide, "kills" Siddhartha the sensualist and businessman, and presents us with a newborn hero ready for a third major development in his life. Through such dramatized incidents, we are brought much closer to Siddhartha and the life of India and grasp the character as more human, the scene as more concrete.

Greater development of the plot's episodes leads to

greater development of character. Brief as is his appearance here, Vasudeva leaves an impression of pleasant simplicity. The peasant girl is a sensual little animal, knowledgeable about such exotic sexual positions as "ascending the tree" (p. 41). Kamaswami is perhaps more a caricature than a character, an Indian Babbitt. He is the "typical businessman": clever, lively, sensual, contemptuous of intellectual skills until he sees Siddhartha's practical success in applying them, astonished and distraught by Siddhartha's unwillingness to give up pleasure for work, subject to continual anxiety about relatively trivial business problems. Still his discomfiture provides some comic touches in this rather solemn book.

Of the secondary characters, Kamala (whose name derives from *Kama*, god of love and the senses as in *Kama Sutra*)[9] receives the greatest development in this part; in fact, only Vasudeva rivals her in importance. Hesse stresses this importance: "Here with Kamala lay the value and meaning of his present, not in Kamaswami's business" (p. 54). Siddhartha's first encounter with the beautiful and intelligent courtesan overwhelms him:

> Beneath heaped-up black hair he saw a bright, very sweet, very clever face, a bright red mouth like a freshly cut fig, artful eyebrows painted in a high arch, dark eyes, clever and observant, and a clear slender neck above her green and gold gown (p. 42).

She is not the villainess of the material world. Although she is a courtesan, she serves the reputable wealthy and maintains a social role which brings her money and status. More important to the novella, she is both coolly observant and sensitive and thus a good vehicle for providing character development of Siddhartha through their interaction and her private observations. In fact, she understands Siddhartha "better than Govinda had once done" (p. 58). She sees before Siddhartha does that he will remain committed always to some need beyond those of the "Kamaswami people" and that he will leave some day.

Kamala has great stature. In their first encounter, after lightly teasing the "stupid Samana from the forest," she reveals that she respects him, for he is like her. Their strength and freedom from others lies in the fact that their most important possessions are talents over which they alone have control: his talent for thought, her talent for love. He returns the compliment, equating her with himself and with Buddha as one of those rare humans who are "like stars which travel one defined path: no wind reaches them, they have within themselves their guide and path" (p. 58). Although one should be a little wary of this kind of praise in the light of the obvious value Hesse places on Siddhartha's becoming "of the people," nevertheless he seems clearly attracted by them to the extent of making Kamala the only other developing character in the book besides Siddhartha himself. Like Siddhartha, she has too much stature to be satisfied with the sensual world. She herself eventually reveals to him the futility of her world, the "weariness from continuing along a long path which had no joyous goal" (p. 65) and is induced by his praise of Buddha to become a convert to Buddhism. When Siddhartha leaves her pregnant with his son, she ceases to be a courtesan. The scene of her death in the third part has power.

Siddhartha's own character becomes even more engaging. Hesse develops dramatically his initial naive, childlike euphoria within nature and among people. In his encounter with Kamala, his combination of simplicity and intelligence is arresting, a mixture further developed as he displays in contrast to Kamaswami the ability of the "impractical intellectual" to be very practical indeed in applying theoretical skills to daily problems—particularly his ability to pursue a single goal until he gains it. Siddhartha's light-heartedness and irresponsibility in the business world while so definitely succeeding in it are engaging victories.

But more compelling than Siddhartha's various successes are his failures. By the middle of the second section these become evident. His aristocratic aloofness is central—the "star" quality which he shares with Kamala. He is separated from the rest of humanity and, most important, really unable to feel, especially to love. It is a failure which leads to his specializing in "passion and power," eroticism and business. He becomes more and more petty, more and more disillusioned. The culminating emotion which Hesse strives to create is nausea.

Siddhartha's nausea is the second stage in the spiritual drama which I find to be the most emotionally powerful element of the book. The transition into nausea is elaborately and carefully managed: the friendliness, the sense of loss of the Samana's spiritual discipline, the mocking superiority he adopts towards the people in his life, the diminishing of his character to childish anxiety, his sense of isolation, his laziness, his irritability and artificiality, his "expressions of discontent, of sickliness, of displeasure, of idleness, of lovelessness . . . . the soul sickness of the rich" (p. 63).

Hesse spends much time on Siddhartha's last stage before total nausea: his addiction to gambling; his recklessness and passion in dicing for money and jewels to display his hostility to wealth through squandering it and to try to arouse "some kind of happiness, some kind of excitement, some heightened living in the midst of his satiated, tepid, insipid existence" (p. 64); his pursuit of more business for the mere purpose of gaining more money for gambling; his spiritual hardening toward others; the grueling effect of the addiction upon him—his physical aging and loss of beauty.

Nausea fully upon him, Siddhartha undergoes a series of "deaths": the death of the game of the world that he had been playing; the death of his pleasure in his possessions; the sense of the death of the Samana in him. His self-disgust is sweeping:

41

He was deeply entangled in Samsara; he had drawn nausea and death to himself from all sides, like a sponge that absorbs water until it is full . . . .

Was there any kind of filth with which he had not besmirched himself, any sin and folly which he had not committed, any stain upon his soul for which he alone had not been responsible (pp. 70–71)?

Spiritually dead, he turns toward physical suicide:

Might the fishes devour him, this dog of a Siddhartha, this madman, this corrupted and rotting body, this sluggish and misused soul! Might the fishes and crocodiles devour him, might the demons tear him to little pieces!

With a distorted countenance he stared into the water. He saw his face reflected, and spat at it. He bent, with closed eyes—towards death (pp. 71–72).

But after such long and deliberate development of Siddhartha's suicidal nausea, Hesse wrenches Siddhartha (and the reader) into a soaring emotional upswing with Siddhartha's hearing of the word *"Om"*:

. . . and he was conscious of Brahman, of the indestructibleness of life; he remembered all that he had forgotten, all that was divine (p. 72).

The tension and despair dissolve instantly into sleep and relaxation, during which he pronounces again and again to himself in a *mantra* the healing word *"Om."* And suddenly he is "remarkably awake, happy and curious" (p. 73). The ensuing conversation with Govinda is lighthearted and amused.

After Govinda's departure, the tone of Siddhartha's

emotions rests somewhere between the troubled (as he thinks of his lost lives as intellectual and as sensualist) and the relieved (as he thinks of his new condition). Appropriately, thought is initially difficult, for he has become "an ordinary person," even a child, "going backwards . . . empty and naked and ignorant in the world" (p. 77). Then comes pressing into his consciousness illumination after illumination and he sees the full implications of his past life. The section ends on a note of happiness, even merriment, and a significant beginning of love for the river near which this spiritual death and rebirth occurred.

Again, the structure of the middle section of *Siddhartha* contributes to and clarifies the development of the hero. "Kamala," the first chapter, makes it clear that Siddhartha realizes that although he has *knowledge* of the world, knowledge is not enough—he must *experience* his knowledge and thus give theory a reality by its practice. Theoretically, for instance, he understands that Atman equates with Brahma (self with universe), but he doesn't *feel* the equation. He must turn to the senses and to human experience. The dream of Govinda (the ascetic intellectual) turning into a woman (the hedonistic sensualist) and of the milk evoking both in its taste, signifies that even at the beginning of the second section of the novella Siddhartha already realizes that thought and sense *together* must be used to find the Way. Finally, Siddhartha also intuits here that the best route to follow is that which a rather mysterious "voice" dictates (as we shall discover, it is the "voice" of the universe speaking through the Self), whether the route be through thought or through senses.

The second chapter, "Amongst the People," stresses Siddhartha's isolation from the rest of humanity—a dilemma that will not be resolved until the third part—and that the "voice" complains of his materialistic life.

The title of the third chapter, "Samsara," needs explanation. Basically, Samsara is reincarnation, a process which the Hindu looks upon as very unpleasant. The word also evokes the impermanent, transitory, unsatisfying world into which man is doomed to be born again and again. The dominant meaning of the word as Hesse uses it is probably that which connotes the unsatisfying quality of this world in which Siddhartha lives as an egotistical individual committed to triviality. It explicitly refers to his sexual life with Kamala, a futile "game without an end . . . . called Samsara, a game for children, a game which was perhaps enjoyable played once, twice, ten times— but [not] . . . worth playing continually" (p. 68). The word also refers to the period of gambling; it is there that Siddhartha's nausea reaches its peak and there that reference is made to a "senseless cycle" of gambling, losing, earning money in business, gambling again, losing again. Another point should be observed in the "Samsara" chapter: Siddhartha's realization of the proximity of "passion . . . to death" (p. 65). Hesse regards the two as related because a life of passion culminates in nothing except a wearying sense of imminent death, for passion offers no sustaining values built as it is upon the transitory body. In other novels he will develop this concept.

It is in the fourth chapter—"By the River"—that Hesse becomes most interested in explicitly developing theme. In fact, near the end of this chapter, appears one of the most important passages in the book—a summary of and commentary on the events so far. Its major point is that in the first section Siddhartha became, as we have seen, an intellectual and in the second a sensualist. The function of the life of the senses, however, was to end his life as a human repressed by conscious intellectual self-discipline. His life among the "Kamaswami people" through despair ended *that* possibility as a single answer. Again, he had to *live* through that life. Since his childhood, the Brahmins had told him that it was a bad one, but he had to find it out for himself; otherwise, the knowledge would have no reality. The product of this double-death of Siddhartha the intellectual and Siddhar-

tha the sensualist is the integration of both into Siddhartha the ordinary man, the child.

At first, it seems to him that he is simply devolving
in an aimless spiral downwards, but then he observes that
what really died and left him feeling like "a child, so
full of trust and happiness, without fear" was

> "his small, fearful and proud Self, with which he
> had wrestled for so many years, but which had
> always conquered him again, which appeared
> each time again and again, which robbed him
> of happiness and filled him with fear" (p. 80).

He could not kill that Self as a Brahmin or a Samana
—though he tried to do so by fasting and self-discipline
—because that aspect of him which forced him into
such acts became the Self which "crawled into this priest-
hood, into this arrogance, into this intellectuality. So to
destroy that strengthening Self in the intellect, he became
one of the "Kamaswami people" with *their* kind of Self,
which in turn burned itself out in "the madness of an
empty, futile life" (p. 81).

The section ends with a clarification of the meaning
of what has passed so far. Its conclusion, however, raises
some questions: Why did the word *Om* have such an
instant curative effect upon Siddhartha? Why does the
river give him such pleasure? What will he do now as a
"child"?

In the last part of the book, Siddhartha, stripped of his
two former spurious selves, finds his true Self: that which
is truly "him" is that in himself which is identical with
that outside himself.

His "private" soul (*Atman*) is really the world soul
(*Brahma*). He discovers that all has been harmonious and
unified and that his sense of being an isolated, searching
individual has been illusory.

To make these points, the plot simplifies considerably.
Dramatized are his first encounter with Vasudeva, the

ferryman, and their decision to live and work together; the death of Kamala; a conversation with Vasudeva about the problems of teaching the willful son; the moment that Siddhartha realizes that he loves his son; the son's final rejection of his father; his anguished vigil at the gate of his son's home; another insight at the river and his subsequent confession to the dying Vasudeva; and the last encounter with Govinda. In terms of simple quantity of developed incidents, this section doesn't differ much from the preceding one, but it approaches the earlier portions of the book in the repetitiveness of the kinds of incidents it dramatizes. Setting aside the episode with the son (not an easy one to "set aside," for it has considerable power), the third section consists largely of dialogues with Vasudeva or internal monologues preparing the reader for the complex thematic developments in the final dialogue that dominates the last chapter, "Govinda."

Characterization is simple also. Kamala has quiet pathos and dignity. Young Siddhartha is simply obnoxious, almost unbelievably so. It is to Hesse's advantage to make Siddhartha and Vasudeva almost indistinguishable: two simple, joyous old men in love with a river because their life near it has shown them the harmony in the universe. Vasudeva elicits intuitions rather than words from Siddhartha; in the end, Vasudeva attains the stature of a gentle, luminous, simple but impressive deity (his name is one of the names for Krishna, in turn an incarnation of one of the three major Hindu gods, Vishnu the Preserver).[10]

Siddhartha becomes distinct from Vasudeva, however, during the episode with his son. Both before and after this episode, he has been aware of the river's main secrets: (1) that if one listens long enough to it, he will hear all of the voices in the universe (that is, in this one phenomenon exists the universe in the river's potential to become all), and (2) that if one listens even more carefully, all the voices blend into one sound, *Om* (that is, underneath this infinite variety and infinite possibility lies one unified being—the whole, *single* universe—as under all the shapes and sounds of the river lies the fact that it is still one thing, a river). But the episode with his son tears from him the joyous equanimity he had gained and will regain. The chapter powerfully dramatizes Siddhartha's gentle, patient, indulgent devotion to his son; his deep love for him despite his knowledge that he can do nothing for the boy except allow him to experience his life as he himself required *his* father allow him to do; his shameless following of the boy; his terrible anguish as he suffers the "wound of love"; his recovery on the day of Vasudeva's death; and his return to his former balance.

The first of the four final chapters, "The Ferryman," underscores the major thematic points. From the river, Siddhartha sees that being can be simultaneously in flux and yet remain the same, as the river can flow and yet remain a river. From it, he learns that there is no such thing as time; the river's beginning, middle, and end are of a single piece like the past, present, and future of Siddhartha's life. From it, he learns that one thing has the potentiality of all things as the river has in its sound all voices and, beyond that, that all things are really different manifestations of one thing—the universal soul that he hears in the *Om* underlying the voices of the river. Thus, when Kamala dies in his arms, though he suffers in the present, he is not damaged by the sorrow, for he sees past and future flow into the present and feels "more acutely the indestructibleness of every life, the eternity of every moment" (p. 93).

But love for his son damages him and does so badly. Not only does Siddhartha have one more human experience to go through—love—and thus join the brotherhood of man, but also Hesse wishes to stress in his last chapter that man's most important act in the universe is the act of love, for it is the act of "joining" together that which in reality has never been apart. The point of Siddhartha's joining the "brotherhood" is that stressed in "The Son." Torn, humiliated, wounded by love, he is finally "reduced" to the level of the ordinary man. Through painful experience once again, he gets inside the reality of humanity and thus shares with it pain and dignity.[11] Again, we can see the difference between the route to wisdom and the route to knowledge.

A brother now to mankind, Siddhartha has erased from his psyche his sense of difference between self and society. Soon he shall erase the sense of difference between self and the whole objective universe "outside" self. Thus in the third chapter, "Om," he confesses his love-wound to Vasudeva, who takes him once more to the river. For the second time, he listens to it; this time, Hesse dramatizes in great detail the voices that Siddhartha hears, so that the moment will have through its dense sound imagery the impact upon the reader that it is to have on Siddhartha. Then when he does not try to listen to any one voice but tries to take them in all at once, he hears the *Om*. At that moment, Siddhartha's "Self . . . merge[s] into unity":

> From that hour Siddhartha ceased to fight against his destiny. There shone in his face the serenity of knowledge, of one who is no longer confronted with conflict of desires, who has found salvation, who is in harmony with the stream of events, with the stream of life, full of sympathy and compassion, surrendering himself to the stream, belonging to the unity of all things (p. 111).

Siddhartha's last goal was to achieve a state of "thinking, feeling and breathing thoughts of unity at every moment of life" (p. 106). He has attained it.

Chapter Twelve, "Govinda," is a clarification, not a development of Siddhartha's final spiritual condition. The passages in this chapter are those in the novella most difficult to grasp. Hesse tells us that what has occurred cannot be grasped by the intellect, that it is futile for Govinda to try to *understand* what can only be *experienced*. Thus, after some efforts to explain, Siddhartha resorts to the metaphor of the stone and, finally, to demonstration; Govinda kisses his forehead and "experiences" Siddhartha's final state of spiritual perfection. The futile explanations, the metaphor, and the demonstration speak clearly enough to that aspect of *us* which experiences rather than understands anything. But our intellects remain somewhat mystified, with various tantalizing questions raised: Why is time not real? Why does there appear behind the transparent mask of Siddhartha's enigmatically smiling face "all present and future forms"? Why is a man who seeks a goal less able to find it than one who doesn't? Why is wisdom incommunicable? Why is a truth that is verbalized only a half-truth? Why must one love things, not words or thoughts? Why is love the most important act in the world? The questions are interrelated; each answer will lead to the next.

But before I wing off into abstractions, I want to make it clear why I feel the last chapter of *Siddhartha* is a beautiful and powerful experience, for it is with my experience of his novella that I am sure Hesse would wish me to begin. Although I always remember the metaphor of the stone when I want to persuade someone to accept Hesse's views, it is the kiss of Govinda that moves me most. What strikes me is the sense of enormous eternal complexities becoming totally *harmonious*. My use of that word must seem obsessive by now, but I must stress that as an agnostic thirty-eight-year-old literature professor consciously experiencing Western history since the 1940's and immersed in the literature of my age and the post-World War I age preceding it, I have believed that not only my society but the very physical universe is in chaos—and that is a belief that has bred in me such pessimism that I badly need a remedy that institutionalized, and dehumanized Christianity is very far from giving me. It is not only restorative for me to discover that Hesse believes that there is some sense, some pattern in the universe, but it is surprising to find that that author believes that that universe involves me in the most extra-

49

ordinary, magnificent way possible: the universe *is* me—
I am the universe. My intellect cannot grasp that paradox
at first, nor can it fully understand the corollary that time
does not exist, but I am *persuaded* by the river and the
stone. Furthermore, I am encouraged in that Hesse tells
me that I need no special talents or learned skills to
become Siddhartha; indeed, Siddhartha's whole direction
was to deprive himself of these and to become a totally
ordinary and childlike person. What Siddhartha managed
was *to see differently* and thus to see what was there
(Hesse assures me and persuades me) to be seen all the
time: that he and I and you and everyone are perfect
because—again the mystifying argument—we are everything and everything is us.

There the novella leaves me, tempted into the beginnings of belief. Now the detestable intellect begins to
grind: "But what does Hesse *mean?*" The main problem
for me is the one that just stopped me: How can *I* be
the universe? Siddhartha's stone goes far to clarify that
point. The stone is not simply one individual stone among
millions, for through its past and its future it has the
potential to become *all* things. To put it another way, the
stone quite simply *does* relate to the universe as a ripple
does to a river: it is a mass of rock becoming mineral
through erosion and other forms of change; that mineral
becomes absorbed into plants and animals, becomes part
of them, and is converted by them into energy; the released energy converts back to mass again, and so on and
on and on. In short, if we could view *quickly* the history
of the stone, we woud see its mass emerge from energy,
curl into form, swirl out into other forms, evaporate into
energy again, and infinitely on and on like the river.
The stone thus "has already long been everything and
always is everything" because it has in it the potential
of being everything. And if it is everything, it is also
perfect because it is *complete* and contains within it all
possibilities—including the possibility of perfection to
such a point that it "impossibly" includes *imperfection*

also; for underneath the infinite flow of being of our stone gleams one great truth: since it has universal possibility, *it is the universe.* Every "thing" is a door through which we pass into infinity and then into the unity of everything.

Thus as is the stone, so is Siddhartha. And so are we. We carry in us every moment our past and our potential. We are *now* what we were and what we can be. We are only prevented from seeing this by our belief in *time,* our belief that somehow the past, the present, and the future are separate. But, Siddhartha says, you can no more separate present from past from future than you can the ripple from the river, the rock from its history, us from the universe. How can we consider ourselves separate from the universe? Where do *I* stop and where does the universe begin? "I" eat and breathe the universe. I take in its mass and energy perpetually and perpetually I restore it: the *whole* mass of my body will completely change through seven years; a gesture of my arm fires into the molecules about me energy which in a chain reaction will someday touch the farthest star. In this sense, then, time doesn't exist: to believe in time is to believe that something which cannot be divided is divided.

If these two points—the identity of self and universe and the nonexistence of time—can be granted, answers to the other five questions come rapidly. A man who seeks a goal is one who seeks something in the universe for Self and thus believes incorrectly that self and universe are two different things; if he would simply "be himself," he would be the universe and the search would end. Second, wisdom is ultimately incommunicable, in the sense that words and verbalized thought are the only means of communication employed; all *analyze,* abstract ideas from things, erroneously break what is whole into "parts" that do not really exist.

Third, the analytical nature of thought and words requires that the intellectual be doomed to half-truths, "one-sided" truths. To make black clear, he must oppose

51

it to white. To make good clear, he must oppose it to evil, for if there were no conception of evil, how could one recognize good? Thus evil is necessary to good, for any course of action that eliminated evil would eliminate good also. The two concepts are just as intimately *related* as they are *opposed*—and that is a reassuring awareness in a world where people stress duality and fragmentation. Let me put this comforting concept in Siddhartha's terms: Since man has the potential of the whole universe, he has the potential in him simultaneously of the greatest evil and the greatest good and all moral shades and circumstances in between. Each *thing* unites in itself that which man's intellect has ignorantly separated into moral ideas.

Fourth, we must love only things because there isn't anything else to love. Last, we must consider that capacity to love our most important ability. It is Siddhartha's last lesson and our most important one, for love unites where the mind divides. Let Siddhartha conclude this last argument with one of the most persuasive passages in the novella:

> Therefore, it seems to me that everything that exists is good—death as well as life, sin as well as holiness, wisdom as well as folly. Everything is necessary, everything needs only my agreement, my assent, my loving understanding; then all is well with me and nothing can harm me. I learned through my body and soul that it was necessary for me to sin, that I needed lust, that I had to strive for property and experience nausea and the depths of despair in order to learn not to resist them, in order to learn to love the world, and no longer compare it with some kind of imaginary vision of perfection, but to leave it as it is, to love it and be glad to belong to it (p. 116).

Siddhartha is a good introduction to the other major novels, for it develops in a simple, schematized structure characters and situations, attitudes and ideas which will repeat themselves throughout Hesse's work—each time with a fresh perspective. For instance, the above-quoted statement is an important thematic key to *Steppenwolf*, *Narcissus and Goldmund* and *Magister Ludi*. Characteristic also are such details as the slow opening followed by more vigorous plot and character development, hostility toward the "Kamaswami" people and the fondness for such intellectual beauties as Kamala, the use of dreams as symbolic keys to character and theme, the delight in nature imagery, the view of the universe as harmonious rather than absurd, the favoring of sense over intellect and of transcendent spirit over both. Hesse's dualism—here expressed in Siddhartha's alternate explorations of the intellect and of the senses—appears in *Steppenwolf* as Harry Haller and the wolf; in *Narcissus and Goldmund* as the titular characters; in *Magister Ludi* as Castalia and the outside world.

Finally, to view Siddhartha's career before those of similar heroes is to get a much clearer perspective on the latter. Siddhartha explains Harry Haller in that Harry only begins the journey that Siddhartha has completed. Goldmund is a specialized Siddhartha—one without success in the intellectual world, but one who "awakens" from such a world, explores the sensual world, and through art arrives at a synthesis of the dualities that he perceives between mind and sense, life and death. Knecht contrasts to Goldmund; he emphasizes the spiritual. *Magister Ludi* explores the unsuccessful effort to wed duality in the intellectual Bead Game; Knecht's journey into the sensual world, however, is short—he dies immediately. Thus, as brief as the novella is, *Siddhartha* gives us the ideal man in the ideal plot making the ideal resolution of the apparently irreconcilable dualities of the world. The reader will never again see Hesse so optimistic as he is in *Siddhartha,* but it may well be that with his country destroyed, his wife insane, his family shattered, his own mind recently unhinged, Hesse never had had such *need* to be optimistic.

CHAPTER TWO

Steppenwolf: Siddhartha Today

Steppenwolf presents a contemporary, Harry Haller, struggling to become a Siddhartha.[1] Tortured by twentieth century dualism, confused by its chaos, Harry progresses disappointingly little in proportion to his great effort. And he is exceptional, a disciplined intellectual whose repeated survival of traumas has given him an unclouded insight into his society. Paralyzed by equal commitments to the moderation and security of the middle class and to a Siddharthian self-realization, all he finally manages is to overcome this conflict to be able to take the first step toward godhood.

In the 1920's, Harry Haller takes a room in a Swiss or German city, where he sporadically explores its literary, artistic, and musical culture. His Germany, torn and traumatized by World War I, is in the political and economic chaos of left-wing revolutions and right-wing counter-revolutions; in Munich, Hitler's aborted putsch is imminent; its repercussions will make him a national figure. But Harry is an outsider. Near fifty, in the preceding years he has made and lost a reputation, watched his wife become insane, attempted suicide, made and lost another reputation as a student of Oriental mysticism, and he now wanders from country to country, friendless except for a beautiful young woman, Erica, whose similar conflicts and isolation have reduced their relationship to infrequent visits ending in violent quarrels. Aimless, unable to work, hating his own self-destructive behavior, Harry now simply browses, writes occasional pacifist articles attacking German militarism, sporadically practices yoga, takes hot baths to ease his neuralgia, drinks heavily, and clutters his room with a chaos of books and pictures. The only cheerful note is his vow to cut his throat on his fiftieth birthday and thus end the hopeless mess.

The events of the novel's first days drive him near this suicide. One evening, mortified by his unwarrantedly wolfish attack on a conventional professor of Oriental mysticism, Harry decides to kill himself but becomes terrified by death. Drunkenly, he stumbles into a tavern where he meets a strange and wise young prostitute, Hermine, who scolds him out of his hysteria. Now Harry begins to mend. It becomes clear that his suicidal nausea, like Siddhartha's, has signalled the end of one personality —the schizophrenic, paralyzed "Steppenwolf's"—and the beginning of another that will see more clearly its internal unity and its harmony with the universe.

Harry's evolution (two-thirds of the novel) is in two stages. First, like Siddhartha, Harry immerses himself in the life of the common people; he learns how to dance, play, laugh, takes another young prostitute as a mistress, and cultivates a friendship with Pablo, a bisexual jazz musician who peddles dope and women on the side. This experience healing what his educated intellect could not, Harry enters the second stage: a psychedelic trip, guided by Pablo through the "Magic Theater," the realm of repressed desires and fears. There he engages in a hilarious guerilla war against automobiles; makes love in endless ways to countless women; sees the disgusting brutality of his battle against himself as a sadistic conflict between a wolf and a man; sees in a fantastic chess game the possibility of endless personalities beyond these two selves; and attacks one of his few remaining heroes, Mozart, who mockingly reveals to Harry the trash-heap of his past. Entering the last room of the Magic Theater and seeing Pablo and Hermine naked in each other's arms, Harry commits what he thinks is the ultimate act of evil; he stabs Hermine, who has come to represent all that he really values, all that has healed him. Seeking punishment with eager masochism, Harry stands trial before his hero Mozart and a jury of other idealized figures. He is convicted and punished; on the count of three Mozart leads his friends in a grand cosmic horselaugh at Harry the Jackass. Mozart becomes Pablo. Hermine shrinks to a toy which Pablo tucks into a pocket. And Harry determines to keep on going through the hell of trying to learn how to love like a Siddhartha—and to laugh like a Mozart.

The aftermath of this amazing and delightful conclusion (one-third of the novel) is reported in the preface by a nameless middle-class observer. It is not as cheering as the novel's final sentences. Eating little and lying in bed all day, Harry goes through another long period of depression. He emerges once to attend with the nameless narrator a historian's lecture; his reaction is sardonic despair at the conceit, superficiality, and futility of modern civilization. He emerges a second time to quarrel violently with Erica (who never appears in the novel) and apparently ends their relationship. Then he leaves and, in the narrator's opinion, will continue to remain a tragic outsider compulsively exploring the hell of his psyche.

Like *Siddhartha's, Steppenwolf's* plot has three sections: (1) an intellectual with intuitions of cosmic harmony finds his knowledge futile; (2) he gains wisdom through experience with the common people; (3) he ultimately experiences a healing vision of universal truth. The first part establishes Harry's paralysis in the eyes of the middle class, the "Immortal," and Harry himself. The second part, beginning with Harry's meeting Hermine, provides wisdom through experience. The third part, beginning with his entry into the Magic Theater, brings the healing vision of the universe through the self. As in *Siddhartha*, there are female and male guides in the second and third parts: Kamala becomes Hermine-Maria; Vasudeva becomes Pablo-Mozart. The most prominent structural difference from *Siddhartha* is that the first part does not rely alone on the central character's self-examination for development; it includes also the "objective" but differing views of Harry by the nameless narrator's preface and the Immortal's "Treatise of the Steppenwolf." I will treat the latter first, for this entertainingly ironic essay not only corrects the self-deceptions of the nameless narrator and Harry but also provides the schema of the whole experience that the novel offers.

Although *Siddhartha* emphasizes eastern mysticism, it also shows the strong influence of western psychoanalysis, specifically that of Carl Jung. It was possible, however, to cover the novella's main ground without reference to Jung. But *Steppenwolf* is a different matter. While I could (and will) explain clearly enough without Jung the central issues of the novel up until Harry's entry into the Fancy Dress Ball, at that point it becomes necessary to understand the theory of personality upon which

Hesse organizes the apparently fantastic incidents of the Ball and the Magic Theater.

Hesse was deeply influenced by Jung, both through having been psychoanalyzed by a Jungian and through conversations with Jung himself—some of which may have occurred during the period of the events in *Steppenwolf*. Jung's object in psychotherapy was to enable the patient to attain *individuation*, that is, to achieve self-realization by bringing together both the conscious and the unconscious worlds, represented in *Steppenwolf* by Harry and the wolf respectively. As long as this synthesis has not been made, the unconscious works independently of and often in conflict with the conscious which ignores its existence. Jung believed not only in Freud's conscious and unconscious, however, but also in two types of unconscious, the personal unconscious, created by the repressed episodes in an individual's history, and the collective unconscious, an inherited memory of central episodes or recurrent conditions in the history of the species. This collective unconscious manifests itself in widespread symbols and figures (*archetypes*) appearing in myths, literature, art.

There are two archetypes, fundamental to Jungian theory, which have a very prominent place in *Steppenwolf:* the *anima* and the Self. Jung believed that each man has a female aspect in his personality; he named this aspect the anima (the opposite applies to each woman; she has an *animus*). Although what each man may consider female in himself may differ from individual to individual, the anima generally contains such qualities as the sensual, the sensitive, the intuitive, the emotional, the irrational. A man represses these in order to develop the logical, rational, practical, mechanical qualities. But, as I said earlier, repressed material in the unconscious will get a life of its own and begin to manipulate the conscious ego. A man forms this female aspect in himself into the image of a woman and projects it on actual women outside him (who are really much more "masculine" than he knows): mother, sister, lover, wife. In a sense, when a man falls "in love" with a woman, he is smitten by one whose special characteristics allow him to see his own feminine nature in her. In short, he falls in love with himself, the repressed self which both attracts and frightens him—there is thus a good deal of truth in the expression, "He has fallen in love with love." Some women have a combination of personal and physical characteristics that correspond to the *archetypal* anima; these are the mysteriously enchanting creatures whom all the world loves. Such, in *Steppenwolf,* is Hermine.

The Self is a human's guide in the enormously difficult task of individuation or self-realization. It is an "inner center" which invents and organizes dreams in order to mirror to the conscious ego the reality of its own hidden nature. In these dreams it will manifest itself in various forms—generally as the same sex of the dreamer. In a male it may become a wise old man like Siddhartha's Vasudeva, or it may become a young vigorous man like Pablo, promising to an older man renewal of energy. It may appear as a hermaphrodite (as does Hermine at times), symbolizing the synthesis of the two elements most at conflict in a human's nature, male and female. It may appear as an animal (the wolf) presenting to the ego the valuable repressed instinctual drives thus far denied. Or it may appear as Siddhartha's stone, symbolizing a unified existence at the farthest distance from the transitory world of the ego, an existence out of space and time—eternal as the Self is eternal and the same.

Whether or not a human matures depends on the extent to which his conscious ego listens to this hidden guide, for it is like a fertilized ovum containing within it all of the potential of the human being that it might become, but yet only a single cell. One of those most unlikely to let the Self become realized is a man like Harry, who is over-conscious, who lives too much in the ego. Of particular use to such people is the anima which, like Hermine, is more attuned to the values and nature of the Self. When a man has struggled long and hard enough with his anima so that he is partially free from that basic human conflict, the unconscious will begin to manifest itself in his dreams as the Self: it will become a man whom he trusts, who will initiate and guard him while he proceeds towards self-realization.[2]

I consider Harry Haller to be Hermann Hesse's conscious ego (note the initials). The "wolf" that Haller thinks he becomes at times is simply his uninformed cover-name for the total unconscious that he is denying. The most prominent elements of that unconscious which begin to emerge as he comes to terms with it are represented by Hermine and Pablo-Mozart. Hermine is the anima (note the first name). Pablo-Mozart is the Self; the Magic Theater is the dream world which the Self invents and organizes to communicate its real nature.

Hesse frequently insisted that his novels were motivated by his own desire to integrate self through the imaginative act, a process that Jung himself recommended as a post-therapy technique. Fresh in Hesse's mind while he was writing this novel must have been the winters (the season of *Steppenwolf*) that he spent in a small apartment in Zurich; he also was undergoing a brief and unhappy marriage with Ruth Wenger, whom he wedded under the compulsion of "life and destiny,"[3] terminology similar to that which Harry uses to describe his relationship with Erica. There is testimony in Hesse's collection of turbulent and inhibited poems, *Krisis*, that in 1926, stifled by ascetic repression and with his second marriage shattered, the author was "engulfed . . . in a vengeful sensuality for almost an entire year"; in these poems, Hesse immerses himself in the world of bars, jazz and sex, yearns to dance and make love; is trapped in conflict between these desires and his conscience; becomes savagely ironic; yearns for death; and finally accepts these conflicts as "God's design, . . . prepared to experience and to exhaust whatever destiny may yet hold in store."[4] In 1927, the long-dead marriage with Ruth was officially ended, *Steppenwolf* was published, and Hesse was recovering from "severe physical exhaustion" to write the calmer *Narcissus and Goldmund*. At this time, he wrote:

> I am now at work on something new and a character is emerging who for a while will serve as symbol and bearer of my life experience. The emergence of these mythical figures (Peter Camenzind, Knulp, Demian, Siddhartha, Harry Haller, and so on) is the creative center from which everything else flows. Almost every book I have written has been a spiritual autobiography.[5]

I don't want to stress the autobiographical or the psychoanalytical elements too much. Hesse's skill lies in submitting these specific insights to the development of beings that have as much to do with all of us as they do with him. He doesn't include the irrelevant from his own life. And he charges Jungian abstractions with the vitality of his powerful imaginative energy. So my procedure will be to explain the novel as long as I can without reference to Jung. That will be until Harry enters the Fancy Dress Ball. Meanwhile, it is quite to Hesse's purpose to have you regard his characters as separate and "real" entities although he will disturb you from time to time with an incongruent bit of fantasy. Don't bother too much about deciding whether or not Hermine is a real person. Hesse's main point is that the great realities of the universe embody themselves in dreams as well as actual people. As "The Treatise on the Steppenwolf" will explain, an assault on those realities on any level, psychological or social, is disastrous.

Central to the "Treatise on the Steppenwolf" is its theory of three levels of consciousness: the middle class, Steppenwolf, and Immortal. The middle class simply wishes to preserve self. It shuns intense experience and absolute positions, follows the middle course between extremes, and seeks peace and physical comfort in bank accounts, strong family ties, support of law and order. For Harry, the symbol of the middle class is the home:

ordered, quiet, clean, comfortable, respectable; the anti-
thesis of the home is the underworld in which Harry
will find wisdom through experience. Respectable, fearful people are very likely to be ruled by dictators, for
they have "substituted majority for power, law for force,
and the polling booth for responsibility" (p. 52).

It is only the Steppenwolf who can preserve the middle
class from itself. The Steppenwolves are those artistic,
spiritual, scientific, or political intellectuals who have
an intuition of the Immortal (Siddharthian) consciousness. Yet they are the sons and daughters of the middle
class and are so trapped by its fears that they believe
that to destroy their inherited conceptions of self would
be suicide. They rationalize that the drive to enter into
the hazardous experience that would ultimately win
them Immortal vision is merely the temptation of the
"wolf" in them, their base animal desires. Although their
intimations of immortality could make them charismatic
guides for the middle class, many (like Harry) are
paralyzed by the conflict between the desire to stay
put and the desire to risk psychic or physical death for
a relevant life that they can find nowhere in the "normal"
society. Only the Steppenwolf who has *humor* can function.

Harry must learn to laugh. He has put himself in an
absurd position. He doesn't have to choose between the
middle-class self in him and the wolf in him, for he is
both (and much, much more besides). Laughter will
reconcile the opposites, heal the split:

> To live in the world as though it were not the
> world, to respect the law and yet to stand above
> it, to have possessions as though "one possessed
> nothing," to renounce as though it were no re-
> nunciation, all these favorite and often formu-
> lated propositions of an exalted worldly wisdom,
> it is the power of humor alone to make effica-
> cious. (p. 55).

Humor replacing the sense of a tragic dualism, the Steppenwolf ceases to be a man-wolf and becomes a unified personality who can begin to experience the infinity of other selves within him. It is *Steppenwolf's* major purpose to demonstrate this need to win unity through a sense of humor that comes from a total self-acceptance. *Steppenwolf* leads us to the cosmic through the comic.

The Immortals possess the third level of consciousness —Siddhartha's. In reality, man does not possess one self or two selves but an infinity of selves. Harry is a double fool for trying to destroy one of his selves: (1) the two-dimensional man is an evolutionary step higher than the one-dimensional middle class; (2) the one route to unity of personality is to so expand it through both ecstatic and terrible experience that it contains not two selves but infinite selves in total harmony. The self then becomes the All. Some have begun to heed this "doctrine of the thousand selves": the "unconditioned" saints and sinners who intensely pursue the absolute regardless of suffering, isolation, self-denial, death. And some of *them*—Mozart and Christ—have become Immortals like Siddhartha through "the power to die, to strip one's self naked, and the eternal surrender of the self" (p. 62).

Of particular value is the Immortal's theory of literature. Working from the premise that as "a body everyone is single, as a soul never" (p. 59), the Immortal author of the "Treatise" advocates a literature which requires the reader "not to regard the characters . . . as separate beings, but as the various facets and aspects of a higher unity . . . of the poet's soul" (p. 60). As I explained in the section on Jung, such a theory would produce a novel in which *all* of the characters were in reality elements of the author's personality manifesting itself in the infinite complexity attainable by all humans. Such a novel employs as "in the Buddhist Yoga an exact technique . . . for unmasking the illusion of the personality" (p. 60). *Steppenwolf* is Herman Hesse. He is potentially the unnamed narrator, Harry Haller, Hermine, Maria, the Immortal Pablo-Mozart, the characters of the Magic Theater. And through this novel, Hesse "unmasks" himself to demonstrate to us our enormous possibilities.

Without the above-described Treatise, the preface would be very deceptive, the evolution of Harry interesting but inconclusive, and the Magic Theater confounding. With it, it is clear that the novel "evolves" along these lines: the point of view of the preface is that of the one-dimensional middle class; that of Harry is the complex and evolving viewpoint of the two-dimensional Steppenwolf; dominant in the last of the novel is the viewpoint of the Immortal. Each reaches to the other, the nameless narrator under the spell of Harry, Harry under that of the Immortal, the Immortal under that of Universal Being.

Through the appropriately nameless narrator of the Preface (hereafter X), Hesse begins his persuasion of the presumably middle class reader and his presentation of a basic element of his own personality by giving $X's$ viewpoint such a fair showing that many of my students have considered it *the* novel's viewpoint until they entered the Magic Theater, whereupon they became puzzled and irritated. Despite the subsequent mockery by the Treatise, X does possess a great many virtues: moderation, psychological stability, practicality, integrity, a good measure of sensitivity and compassion, and intellectual curiosity accompanied by keen and intelligent observation.

Yet those students who find themselves more Steppenwolf than middle-class are put off by an undertone created by the implications of $X's$ statements. Explicitly, his spying on Harry's private life is unpleasant; X himself feels guilty. Implicitly negative in the terms of this novel are his prudishness about Harry's drinking and smoking, his neurotic dislike of disorder, his insecure reaction to the slightest possibility of criticism or condescension, his snobbish esteem of education and the symptoms of prosperity. His life is structured against intense experience and true self-realization.

But X's fear, sterility, and dull existence come from his assumptions about man, not from any innate incapacity to perceive. He believes that Harry's life demonstrates that the universe is ultimately absurd, chaotic, and tragic. Originally suspicious of Harry, X begins to respond to Harry's charisma (demonstrating the value of the Steppenwolf to the middle class): a combination of a very human emotional sensitivity, an occasional child-like gaiety, and a trained mind which is keen, objective, and free from pretension. The human and the childlike qualities ease X's fears. The intellect leads X to condemn modern intellectual superficiality, vanity, and aimless hyperactivity. Ultimately, he sees Harry as a tragic hero, a representative of the best in humanity caught in the chaos and conflict of a major transitional period in human history and striving futilely to reconcile in himself the warring forces of the stable past and the alien, volatile future.

To X, Harry's tragic flaw is his hatred of self. The Steppenwolf is "ailing," incapable of altruism because of a self-hatred that "is really the same thing as sheer egoism, and in the long run breeds the same cruel isolation and despair" (p. 11). The Immortal would agree, but for different reasons; whereas X deplores the destruction of a middle-class self which preserves through fearful moderation a state of minimal awareness and vitality, the Immortal would deplore a self-contempt that prevented Harry from accepting the wolf in him and moving on into the infinite possibilities of being that come to the true self. For the Immortal, Harry's "tragic flaw" is a comic blunder.

The narrator can carry us no further than this: man has the options of stoic self-stultification or a painful engagement with reality that can lead only to suicide. It would seem at the end of the preface that X has begun to lean toward the latter alternative:

> I think of him often. He has not made life lighter for me. He had not the gift for fostering

strength and joy in me. Oh, on the contrary! But
I am not he, and I live my own life, a narrow,
middle-class life, but a solid one, filled with
duties. And so we can think of him peacefully
and affectionately, my aunt and I (p. 20).

I prefer to believe, however, that the narrator has begun
to find the wolf in himself, that as he is what Harry (and
Hesse) was, so he will begin to become what Harry is
and will be. But even if the narrator doesn't evolve,
certainly the viewpoint of the novel does. The next attitude that the reader must experience is that of the
trapped Steppenwolf.

Hesse introduces *Harry Haller's Records* in three-parts:
(1) the presentation of Harry as the man-half of the
Steppenwolf, (2) "The Treatise on the Steppenwolf"
futilely explaining Harry to himself, (3) the presentation
of Harry as wolf compulsively destroying just as the
Treatise predicted. The introduction ends with Harry's
meeting with Hermine in the Black Eagle, whereupon
he begins to live, to enjoy, and to evolve. Thus the parts
before and after the Treatise dramatize passages in it,
largely its first section, the definition of the Steppenwolf.
   The Treatise explains that Harry is in conflict with his
animal nature, which he symbolizes as a wolf providing
to his character a love of freedom, a social independence,
strength and a dangerous savagery, a lust for blood and
sex. Harry the man is moral, clever, interesting to others,
refined, engaged in high thoughts, fine emotions, and
good acts. Accordingly, he has alienated all who have
loved him, for when he reveals his full personality to
those closest to him, those who loved the man are shocked
by the wolf while those who loved the wolf are even
more put off by the man. At rare moments these two
characteristics and all that they represent—feminine and
masculine, happiness and suffering, god and the devil—
harmonize to produce an ecstatic vision of the universal

67

and the eternal. But this vision simply creates another set of poles between which Harry oscillates: a view of life as a bad joke opposed to a view of man as an immortal child of the gods. Harry accordingly is isolated both by an inclination for independence and loneliness ("Steppenwolf" implies "lone wolf") and by society's rejection of him. Whereas the isolation has had the value of allowing him to evolve out of the one-dimensional middle class, the lack of human relationships has produced suffocation, stultification, despair, and ultimately a suicidal nausea. Yet this suicidal tendency has its values. Harry's determination to kill himself on his fiftieth birthday makes his dilemma less of a trap and allows him to continue life. Although Harry's desire to kill himself is perhaps contemptible, the end that he seeks by suicide is laudable: Harry wants to go "back to the mother, back to God, back to the all . . . to be extinguished and to go back to the beginning" (48). But he must do so by living:

> The way to innocence, to the uncreated and to God leads on, . . . not back to the wolf or to the child, but ever further into sin, ever deeper into human life (pp. 63-64).

To become whole again, Harry must embrace life in all its magnificence and horror, beauty and foulness, order and chaos, ecstasy and suffering. One half of existence cannot be without the other, for opposites create themselves.

But Harry is far from this last realization. In the pre-Treatise material, we see him as the man-half thinking fine and beautifully melancholy thoughts about his idyllic childhood, his romantic youth, about the beauties of nature, about art, architecture, literature, and philosophy; and we see him denying the world he lives in: its machine culture, its intellectually and emotionally impoverished people, its easy amusements. But his life, consisting this day of isolated idleness in his room and a lonely walk to and back from a bar, is worse in its sterility, its contentment, its uneventfulness than is the deepest anguish; his boredom produces in him a suicidal nausea and the wolfish desire to smash, destroy, turn order into anarchy.

In the post-Treatise material, the wolf makes its appearance. It angrily mocks at the hypocritical mourners at a funeral. It allows Harry to accept a dinner invitation from a former colleague who hasn't yet learned of the shocking events of Harry's past: his lost profession, lost income and reputation, his wife's insanity and his divorce, the hatred of his neighbors, the years of wandering, suffering and guilt. But then the wolf arises again; it grins at the sentimental, lying Harry, faces him with his hypocrisy. At the professor's house, the wolf is offended by the trivial and soulless furnishings, the vapid complacency of the professor and his wife, and is infuriated by the professor's criticism of an article against German militarism which, unknown to him, was written by Harry. At dinner, Harry begins by lying politely. Then nausea sets in. Then a wolfish humor emerges, upsetting the host. Finally the wolf bares "his teeth in a grin" and savagely attacks the conceit, sentimentality and pomposity of the professor's life. Harry whiningly apologizes: he isn't fit for people, is drinking too much, is ill, is bad-tempered, was the one who wrote the offensive article. But the wolf rears again and attacks Germany for its mad policies of war. Humiliated and defeated, the last of his acquaintances gone, Harry stumbles out into the night; he can't love the middle class and must impotently attack them, he can't love himself, he is lonely, he is trapped, he has lost everything, he is in agony, he can't return to his lonely room and face himself, he must leave town, must run again. He will kill himself. But upon this thought, enormous fear arises; he dreads death as much as he dreads life. Drunkenly, he stumbles from tavern to tavern until he enters the Black Eagle.

The "golden track" has led Harry to the Black Eagle. As the Treatise observed, the Steppenwolf's paralysis was not complete: it has been relieved from time to time by ecstatic visions of a magnificent and meaningful universe, eternal and whole, that could appear to him as if by magic one day. He has seen this "golden track" in moments of communion with nature and with the souls of the great artists, philosophers, and musicians—particulary Goethe and Mozart. He saw it in the episodes connected with the Treatise: the beautiful ancient wall with its fantastic sign inviting madmen into the Magic Theater; the signboard man's gift of the Treatise; and the encounter at the funeral where the man told him, "Go to the Black Eagle, man, if that's what you want" (p. 74). Now he finds it in Hermine. He walks directly to her, she says exactly the right things to him, and she soothes him to sleep where he has a restoring dream of Goethe.

As Harry is to realize later, the professor's Goethe portrait upset him because he saw *himself* in it: *he* has so far drifted from himself that he has become pompous, vain, and, especially, dishonest (he won't die for his pacificism; he detests capitalism but holds stock; he praises man's courage and vitality but huddles in middle-class homes in fear of disorder, accident, and death). He has posed as "a spiritual champion whose all-too-noble gaze shone with the unction of elevated thought and humanity, until he was almost overcome by his own nobleness of mind" (p 130). Goethe was a true "spiritual champion," a man who knew personal anguish and humanity's great failures and yet preached "faith and optimism" and—even more—practiced it through his "unconditioned and self-willed determination to live" (p. 96). And he was "enchantingly alive": in the dream he plays with Harry, teasing him like a child; he dances most uninhibitedly and beautifully to the magnificent music of those who composed his songs; and he has loved many women, as is suggested by the allusions to his mistress, Christiane Vulpius, to the poet Bürger's Molly, who is suspected to be on the premises, as well as to the delightful miniature woman's leg he sports. Above all, he laughs, for he is an Immortal.

70

Harry can only respect the lofty half of Goethe. But Hermine will teach him to be the whole man. He comes to her to ask her to free him from his terrible tension; he can neither live nor die. He wants to be able to do one or the other. She will teach him to do both. Harry is so incapable of action, so caught between life and death, that he is like a child. So Hermine becomes a mother and obtains from him the obedience that the helpless man is more than willing to give, for "she treated me exactly in the way that was best for me at that moment, and so she has since without an exception" (p. 86). She intuits his suicidal intention, mocks him as a baby, feeds him, gives him wine, polishes his glasses, scolds him, overrides his feeble protests, orders him to sleep (whereupon he dreams his healing dream of Goethe), all in a voice "deep and good and maternal" (p. 93). She leaves him because he cannot dance with her, because he does not have the courage to try, and because he does not have the self-confidence to ask her to stay with him. He responds with great anxiety: his only support may collapse; he will again be left to face himself in his lonely room.

Hermine reassures him that she will stay if he will learn how to dance. At home, X's aunt becomes another mother who, like Hermine, urges him not to be so inhibited, to "live as best pleases you and do as best you can" (p. 102). He finds himself suddenly relaxed and easy with her, open in speaking about himself, and free from painful bitterness about his old targets, science and modernism. Hermine has brought him her understanding, for she committed the same follies as he; he is no longer isolated, there are people like him, he is *understood*. Harry is ceasing to be a lone wolf. Unknown to him now at that moment in the Black Eagle he performed precisely the same service for Hermine.

Now Hermine must teach Harry to dance. If he was like a child at first, he was a bad child: naive, helpless, petulant, selfish, full of foolish fears, "too lazy to learn to dance . . . too lazy to learn to love" (p. 128). Dancing

71

will restore the valuable qualities of childhood, those of Goethe's childlike "curiosity and love for idleness and play" (p. 96), her own happy childlike ability to live for the moment and within those moments to make "rapid changes from the deepest seriousness to the drollest merriment, and this without doing herself the least violence, with the facility of a gifted child" (p. 107). The wolf also has virtues:

> You can't help seeing that all of them are right. They're never in any embarrassment. They always know what to do and how to behave themselves. They don't flatter and they don't intrude. They don't pretend. They are as they are . . . (p. 114).

It was the composure and the beauty of the animal in him that had attracted Hermine in the Black Eagle.

Through dancing, Hermine challenges Harry's intellectuality: it has isolated him so that he "can see nothing and read nothing any longer in the eyes of other men" (p. 108); it has made him believe that while he has not learned the simpler lessons of life, his mind has "tested life to the bottom and found nothing in it" (p. 88); it makes him impatient with other men who have rested content with values that he doesn't understand because he doesn't realize that dancing "is every bit as easy as thinking, when you can do it, and much easier to learn" (p. 119).

Harry's inability to obey when Hermine commands him to dance at the Black Eagle is evidence to him that living is much harder than dying. But it isn't. Hermine rapidly teaches the old Steppenwolf, appropriately, the fox trot. On the first day, he is somewhat stiff and clumsy, steps on her toes, makes her laugh at this inhibited intellectual's lack of that which life easily gives: "gaiety, innocence, frivolity, elasticity." He learns the step the second session, though, and learns also, with horror, that he— the "elderly, shy, touchy crank" (p. 120)—must really dance the next day at the Balance Hotel. Fearfully rehearsing that night in his stocking feet to the tinny music of an obnoxious phonograph amid his pictures and poetry, he feels far from ready for the next day. But attracted by the blonde, beautiful, happy Maria, so "gay and certain" in her dancing, and urged by Hermine to try his fox trot out on her, he does. With Maria, he stops reacting to the dance with his mind and does so with his body instead, enchanted by her erotic touch and guided by movement instead of words. Dancing is as easy as living . . . and living is quite easy, quite possible. Soon, like Goethe, he will be able to caper "joyfully and nimbly up and down . . . to and fro with his dance steps and figures" (p. 97).

Dancing is an appropriate metaphor for Hesse to use. It not only applies to the spontaneity of life, a non-verbal act and communication enacted by doing rather than thinking; it is also related to music, and thus to Mozart (to whose tunes Goethe dances) and thus to the Immortals. Music is of central concern to Harry—and to Hesse. From Mozart and Bach the intellectual Harry first intuited the presence of the Immortals, their serene laughter, their existence in a timeless eternity, the radiant, cool, clear quality of that existence. It is to the music of Pablo (who will become Mozart in the Magic Theater) that he now dances. Pablo maintains that music, even intellectual music, begins with humans making it and humans loving it; whether high or low, eternal or transient, it guides, comforts, and inspires *humanity*. Maria further shows Harry that the quality of her response to Pablo's music is as deep, exalted, and honest a response to beauty as is the most sophisticated intellectual's. Yet just before he beds Maria, Harry regrets that the compelling mixture of the intellectual and the sensual has lured German intellectuals away from practical applications of the mind so that the businessman and the general rule the world.

Harry's lessons in living are not yet complete. Hermine begins her last lesson by teaching Harry love—not the "ideal and tragic love" he has painfully felt for the irritable and equally constrained Erica. Instead, he must "learn to love a little in an ordinary human way" (p. 128); he must simply sleep with a pretty girl. The effects of a night in bed with Maria are miraculous: his faith in the beauty and value of music is restored; he becomes aware of the rich life of the senses; he begins to see the beauty and taste of the lives of the common people and the possibility that, as well as the intellectual, they can produce Immortals; most important, he begins to see the beauty of his own past life, its valid emotions, its beautiful women, "riches, riches to be proud of." His life attains "purpose and character and turned not on trifles, but on the stars" (p. 141). He can now "recognize chance as destiny once more and see the ruins of my being as fragments of the divine"; he may be able to gather the "scattered images" of his personality, unify the wolf and the man, and "enter . . . into the world of imagination and be immortal . . . the goal set for the progress of every human life" (p. 142). Harry has jettisoned his ever-present middle-class guilt about sex, entered the garden of innocence, and become fully a child, a dancing child, to delight in "life's surface play, to pursue a fleeting joy, and to be both child and beast in the innocence of sex" (p. 157).

Hermine's lesson is taught. Next Harry and Hermine will learn together. Harry no longer wants death out of fear of life; he has learned to live and enjoy life. But gentle hedonism is not enough. Maria is a summer flower, who will fade. Sensuality merely pacifies the wolf and gives Harry strength for a nobler effort. He senses that Hermine meant Maria as "a prelude and a preparation . . . everything was pushing eagerly forward . . . the gist of the matter was to come" (p. 147).

Restored to the garden of innocence, now Harry must fall again—the right way. The fall is in four stages, from the peak of his life to its depth. The first stage down—although it doesn't seem like it at this point of the novel—is his transcendence of Hermine's femininity through a vision of the eternal. This vision is true and powerful enough, but only half of the picture and a half regarded altogether too seriously for a man who must learn how to laugh at his own pretensions. The second stage is the necessary farewell to Maria and the garden of innocence. The third is a farewell to his old life in the limbo of disillusioned drinkers at the Steel Helmet. The fourth is a vision that makes him furious: the new crucifixion—Moses flattened out in a third-rate movie. When Harry enters the Fancy Dress Ball, he is back where he started.

The day before the Fancy Dress Ball, Harry and Hermine have a long conversation. His lesson in life is over; he has rejected a purposeless sensual life as he had before rejected a purposeless death. He tells Hermine that he too now seeks "to suffer with eagerness and lust after death" (p. 148). She understands. She believes that their lives are those of people who "have a dimension too many" (p. 151); astonished, he learns that had she not met him that night at the Black Eagle, she might have killed herself for the same reasons (a doubly-significant statement if we consider Hermine as Harry's anima). Both were human beings who sought to know Self fully only to find that the more they achieved this, the more isolated from others they were and the more purposeless their lives became. Both had once had high goals but found that they lived in a world that demanded nothing, no sacrifice, no dedication:

> Whoever wants music instead of noise, joy instead of pleasure, soul instead of gold, creative work instead of business, passion instead of foolery, finds no home in this trivial world of ours—
> (p. 151).

Hermine believes that all but a few men have always felt this way. Those few, the true seekers of Self, the dedicated ones, the performers of true acts and true feelings, the lovers of music, joy, soul, creativity, and

75

passion, only find death. Both Harry and Hermine seek that death.

At this point, Hesse develops through Hermine a strange vision of the world into which Harry and Hermine might enter through their deaths. Its central condition is that it is timeless, for it is in eternity: "And eternity was nothing else than the redemption of time, its return to innocence . . . and its transformation again into space" (p. 154). Our world of "time and appearances" is an illusion; the eternal world is *the* reality, populated by those beings, the Immortals, who lived life as it really was—the few humans who lived the truth of the universe as did Siddhartha, living lives that demanded great effort, pain, fearlessness of death, dedication to the most painful search that any man can embark upon: the honest search for Self, which discovers in Self the universe through an infinite expansion of Self through cycles of life and death, of successive personalities. This world "behind time" is for Hermine, who was once a Christian, "a golden heaven, shining, beautiful and full of peace" (p. 153); it contains Christ and the saints whom she loved so well. For Harry, it is "crystalline," lit by starlight in "radiant serenity," a "quivering . . . clearness of ether," and cold: "time frozen into space, and above it there quivered a never-ending and superhuman serenity; an eternal, divine laughter." The laughter is "the laughter of the immortals . . . laughter without an object . . . simply light and lucidity":

> It was that which is left over when a true man has passed through all the sufferings, vices, mistakes, passions and misunderstandings of men and got through to eternity and the world of space (p. 154).

In it live Harry's Mozart and Goethe, "enraptured, refashioned."

Harry has, through his conversation with Hermine, formed a complete spiritual identification with her and

76

all she immediately represents—the spontaneity of the child, life, love, beauty, the intuitive, the female as mother and sister. He has transcended her femininity and perceived her as a being identical with him spiritually. Especially important to him in this identification is their shared belief in eternity:

> I needed it, for without it I could not live and neither could I die. The sacred sense of beyond, of timelessness, of a world which had an eternal value and the substance of which was divine had been given back to me today by this friend of mine who taught me dancing (p. 154).

Next, Harry parts with Maria. Their last night of love-making is their fullest. But it is not enough. Harry seeks more: "another bid for the crown of life in the expiation of its endless guilt. An easy life, an easy love, an easy death—these were not for me" (pp. 157-8). His mood now is Christ-like: to attain eternal life, he will suffer.

The next day, Harry has forgotten his sense of eternity and Maria and Hermine. He sleeps all day, as he used to, and remembers the ball only at the last moment. Alone, he enters the long-deserted Steel Helmet and meets once again his old companions, "the bent and dreaming drinkers, those disillusioned ones, whose brother I had been for so long" (p. 160). The wolf no longer snarling at Harry's "sentimentality," he bids a silent goodbye to his old life with a "feeling of change and decay and of farewell celebrations" (p. 159).

Harry's last preparation is an accident. Still procrastinating, he enters a theater where he sees to his surprise a film about Moses leading the Israelites out of Egypt. Here is another Immortal, a hero with whom Harry identifies, the being who, in Harry's childhood, gave him "the first dawning suspicion of another world than this" (p. 161). It is a reminder to him of eternity and his mission. But simultaneously it recalls and brings into malignant psychic activity all of the disappointments and frustrations with which society confronts the dedicated. Not only does he see the godlike Moses pursued by the Egyptians, deserted by the hedonistic Israelites as he faces God alone, but he watches all of this in a *film*, having a cash value on it, presented to people who will be lost in wonder at the trick photography, eating food complacently, unaffected. Harry is infuriated by the audience and its "dismal pretence of dying by inches" (p. 162).

His "secret repressions and unconfessed fright" amplified by the experience of seeing once more how useless to humanity are its Immortals, Harry enters the masked ball in the old mood of frustration, anger, fear, inhibition, and absolute isolation that had accompanied him for so many years. It is clear that he has not yet solved his problems; he has only prepared himself for a solution. In the ballroom he becomes totally excluded from the "dancing and music and laughter and tumult" of this microcosm of society: "artists, journalists, professors, business men, and of course every adherent of pleasure in the town" (pp. 162-3). He sits drinking among strangers, ignores the girls who ask him to dance, cannot even get drunk. And he becomes aware "that the Steppenwolf was standing behind me with his tongue out" (p. 163). Angry, he begins to leave: "It was surrender and backsliding into my wolfishness, and Hermine would scarcely forgive me for it" (p. 163). Harry has fallen.

Now Jung will become useful. Recall the three basic elements of the male personality: the conscious ego (or Harry), the anima (Hermine), the Self (Pablo-Mozart). Keep in mind that a basic male problem is projecting one's own feminine characteristics on women, that such resultant conflicts are a major bar to man's learning more about the Self, that ego must integrate anima (to be accomplished by "killing" Hermine), that anima is that aspect of the personality closer to Self because more in the unconscious (thus Hermine guides Harry to Pablo-Mozart). And keep in mind that I will try not to apply

78

these concepts too mechanically as I use them to illuminate the Fancy Dress Ball and the Magic Theater.

Inevitably my remarks on the climactic sections of *Steppenwolf* will fall as short of the reality of the book as an anatomical illustration does of a man. To make clear to the conscious what Hesse makes clear to the whole psyche will require regarding the book as more of a mechanism than as the organism that it is. I will isolate mechanical operations of ego, anima, and Self as they from time to time emerge clearly from the flow of Hesse's narrative. But they all synthesize in one man. They merge and exchange identities more and more as the ego begins to realize it is part of the anima and vice versa and, more confusing yet, as the Self appears variously as ego, anima and infinite other beings.

So, inevitably, I will be making Harry's mistake: I will be considering the characters and that which they symbolize as *parts* instead of as the whole variously manifesting itself to an uninformed and unintegrated part, the ego, Harry. It is a legitimate enough approach insofar as the novel appears to us through Harry's point of view, but the main character is finally Hesse, not Harry. This fact will become clear as Hesse in creating the Magic Theater begins to free himself from the bondage of his own ego. Actually, this freeing of ego has already occurred in a more subtle, because more familiar, sense with the Hermine episodes. But, in the Magic Theater, Hesse enters imaginatively into more alien psychic country.

My emphasis so far has been on the rewarding developments in Harry's character. Now, with Jung in mind, I want to examine Hermine. Throughout Hermine's education of Harry into life, there has been a subtle evolution of her character. She developed him by consecutively becoming those women upon whom his earliest anima projections would have been fixed—and in chronological order. She has been both mother and childhood friend and sister.

Her role as mother is quite obvious. When Harry

79

stumbled drunkenly out of the dark into the light and confusion of the Black Eagle, he underwent a symbolic birth trauma, for Hermine instantly and persistently mothers him, calling him "baby" over and over. In the broader sense, there is birth of another sort: through the pale, attractive prostitute Hermann Hesse gives birth to his own female self, the *anima* emerging in the role he first projected it upon, as his mother.

Hermine soon gains another role: sister, companion of childhood days about which Harry and Hermine are later to speak during the dance in "Hell":

> . . . those years of childhood when the capacity for love, in its first youth, embraces not only both sexes, but all and everything, sensuous and spiritual, and endows all things with a spell of love and a fairylike ease of transformation such as in later years comes again only to a chosen few and to poets, and to them rarely (pp. 166-7).

At this stage of their relationship, Harry also sees Hermine as a once-loved male, his boyhood friend Herman, "the enthusiast, the poet, who had shared with ardor all my intellectual pursuits and extravagances" (p. 125). Jungian symbols for the Self are the child (the original Self still not fragmented) and the hermaphrodite (male and female elements united). Hermine, now Herman, has become both; because the ego has not yet had to adopt a "male" role, there is no necessity for it to project its femininity upon a female. The result is a feeling of the integration of Herman's feminine emotionality and poetic nature with Harry's intellectuality. But as acceptable as Hermine is at this stage, Harry can't approach her physically; he can dance with Maria, but not her. Between them are the masculine taboos: the bans against incest (with mother/sister) and homosexuality (with loved male) with which puberty turned him out of the innocence of his childhood.

Harry can, however, cultivate the certain positive aspects of his anima. He can merge with Hermine on the spiritual level, can wed her art of living to his knowledge of life, can be led by her "to dance and play and smile" while he teaches her "to think and know" (p. 126). The man is guided by his anima to the lost world of the mother, of erotic love, earthly life and beauty, music, laughter, play, and the dance; and he leads her to the world of the father, "the spirit, the Logos, the Word" (p. 135). The night before the Ball, Harry can see beyond Hermine as woman; he sees her as a human being, as himself, as an element of his personality just as dedicated to self-individuation as he is (the anima of the unconscious yearns for the same goal of wholeness as does the man of the conscious), as having suffered the same trials as he, as being able to see the same eternity, the same wholeness as he does, as attracted as he to the doctrine of the thousand souls. On the spiritual plane, Hesse can accept all of his abstractly female characteristics as of great human value.

In the descent into "Hell" at the Fancy Dress Ball, Harry challenges even the taboos of incest and homosexuality that bar him from Hermine. A card, inviting him to the Magic Theater and announcing that "HERMINE IS IN HELL," brings him out of paralysis. He eagerly descends to a basement room decorated as Hell, where he will undergo a purgation and a purification that prepare him for the consciousness-shattering experiences of the Magic Theater.

Hesse now confronts the male and female elements of his personality with one another quite overtly; in one of the most compelling episodes of the novel, Hermine meets Harry as Herman, and they recall together the period of youthful eroticism when they loved "all and everything" (p. 167). They compete for the same girls, relating to them sexually as either man or woman, and the consciousness of Harry finally subsides in "the mysterious merging of the personality in the mass, the mystic union of joy"; he is "intoxicated and released from the self . . . half-crazed," possessed by the "deep and childlike happiness of a fairy tale," no longer differentiating himself from the orgiastic mass of people whirling about him (pp. 168-9).

The crowd dwindles as his intoxication increases. Self obliterated, defenses lost, inhibitions destroyed, Harry is now prepared for Hermine. The two elements of Hesse's psyche are ready to merge on all levels. Incestual and homosexual fears vanish; the bodies of Harry and Hermine meet in the "nuptial dance" of the combining physical and spiritual being. Whether Hesse merged thus with a real woman or whether he attained imaginatively a merging and full acceptance of that which Harry and Hermine represent, his accomplishment was indeed rare; he passed the barrier before which most of humanity halts in frustration—the illusion that man is man and woman is woman. They are not. As male or female, they are fragments. United beyond sex, they are human.

As magnificent and unusual an accomplishment as it is, the transcending of the barriers between the male ego and its anima is not enough. Closer to the Self and its greater needs, Hermine intuited this fact long ago in the Globe Rooms while Pablo played dance music:

> I am going to teach you to dance and play and smile, and still not be happy. And you are going to teach me to think and to know and yet not be happy (p. 126).

The ego and the anima are merely parts of the total Self, "unhappy children . . . fallen out of nature and . . . suspended in space" (p. 126).

Since the meeting in the Black Eagle, death has been an undertone of Hermine's characterization as well as Harry's. In her first appearance, she and her world of Eros are associated with death; she is pale and wears "a withered flower in her hair," a camellia, associated perhaps with another courtesan who died for her lover, Dumas' "The Lady of the Camellias." Shortly after, in his Goethe dream, Harry is alternately attracted and horrified by a miniature female leg which keeps turning into a scorpion, itself associated at the beginning of the dream with Vulpius, Goethe's mistress.[6]

The association of love and death becomes more explicit in their second encounter. Appearing to Harry as "a magic mirror," Hermine becomes the hermaphrodite, both girl and his boyhood friend, Herman, the "enthusiast, the poet, who had shared with ardor all . . . intellectual pursuits and extravagances" (p. 125). In this guise of the wedded ego and anima, Hermine tells him that once she has taught him life, she will make him fall in love with her, and then:

> "When you are in love with me I will give you
> my last command and you will obey it, and it
> will be the better for both of us. . . . You won't
> find it easy, but you will do it. You will carry
> out my command and—kill me"(p. 110).

Their life together, as valuable as it will be, must end in a "death" to make room for greater maturation. Her face at this moment becomes a "mask" (p. 108), Jungian symbol of the ego, now an ego with anima integrated into it but yet one "masking" the rest of Self which remains unrealized. Both seek this death, a death of separate male and female selves and a birth of a sexually unified being, and then the death of that being and another rebirth, and so on through death and birth through the thousand selves to the unified Self beyond the time of death and birth in the eternity of timeless space, the realm of the Immortals, those who have won unity with the universe.

Such a death is no horror; in fact, it even makes the present moments of erotic life much more valuable:

> "Do we live to abolish death? No—we live to
> fear it and then again to love it, and just for
> death's sake it is that our spark of life glows for
> an hour now and then so brightly" (p. 118).

What they have done together up until now—including Harry's full exploration of the world of the anima in the Magic Theater—has been positive. But in the mathematics of the psyche, a positive taken to its extreme becomes a negative. Harry in part had arrived at this fact with Maria and turned from purposeless sensuality to the greater spiritual values of the anima at the moment before the Ball when he and Hermine together contemplated the world of the eternal. But Harry did not see that he would have to move beyond—way beyond—Hermine to enter that world; thus he will later turn his back on the "fairy tale" of the Magic Theater to find her and present himself as "the completed man" (p. 203). But because he wants only her, he is so far from completion that instantly he will fall. Then he will murder her.

So when the Ball ends:

> somewhere, at an indeterminable distance and height . . . was a laugh, made of crystal and ice, bright and radiant, but cold and inexorable (pp. 172-3).

The immortal laughs at Harry's minor achievement. Harry faces the anguish of such terrible and ecstatic unions with a thousand other souls. The Magic Theater is open.

When Hermine leads Harry to the Magic Theater, Hesse begins to drive himself and us through the complex experiences of the ·evealed Self, to create the humor and the horror, the variety, the richness, the fantastic and magic nature of the inner world which promises to free us, renew us, and complete us. Above all, through its bizarre comedy and through the ironies and pranks of Pablo/Mozart, the Magic Theater conveys to the somber and tragic mystic Harry the quality and vitalizing value of humor, the humor that returns him to the world and arms him for its difficulties and for the future trials of exploring the Self within him. Thus Pablo's tone will be like that of the "Treatise" and like that conveyed by Siddhartha's ambiguous smile: "perhaps gracious, perhaps mocking."

Appropriately, Pablo has so far appeared to Harry as a subordinate person in the world of Hermine—as a good-looking, childlike, vigorous, empty-handed, sexually potent young musician dabbling in the forbidden worlds of the pimp, the homosexual, and drug pusher. His eyes particularly have fascinated Harry; they have smiled but were vacant (the vacancy of the unknown Self or the vacant gaze of a God?). Then they become the eyes of an animal (the wolf flickers past) but unlike an animal's eyes, they laugh (as does the Immortal); now they become the eyes of a witch, erasing reality (like Hermine) and now they become a mirror to the "lost and frightened" Harry. They are black eyes reflecting the night of the Self as the gray eyes of Hermine reflected the midway region between Harry's world and Pablo's.

Suddenly articulate and intelligent, Pablo gives Harry the drugs that will lead him to the eternal world that he covets so much: it is within himself.[7] Then he gives Harry two other mirrors. The first reflects the ego's vision: the two merging and separating shapes of man and wolf, "unutterably sad . . . self-tormented . . . frightened," angry. Far from being savage, the wolf is "shy, beautiful, dazed"—a creature attractive to a Harry led by Hermine into the world of the child and the animal (p. 175). Conducting Harry to the Magic Theater, Pablo shows him the mirror of the two-dimensional man again so that he can commit "a trifling suicide" (destroy the ego-conception of self) (p. 177); it is not a permanent suicide— Harry will probably become a Steppenwolf again, but a better-educated one. Yet it momentarily releases Harry to envision the real Self, which he finds in a "gigantic mirror" revealing the delightfully comic images of a thousand merry Harrys: "youths, boys, schoolboys, scamps, children . ."; fifty-year-olds leapfrogging twenty-year-olds, thirty-year-olds, five-year-olds "solemn and merry, worthy and comic, well-dressed and unpresentable, and even quite naked, long haired, and hairless" (p. 179). They bounce around, in and out of the mirror; a laughing homosexual Harry leaps into Pablo's arms and goes off with him.

Harry is ready for the Magic Theater, "a jolly one" with "lots to laugh at" with an infinite number of doors leading to an infinite number of rooms, within each a life for one of Harry's infinite souls. Pablo directs Hermine to the right of the theater and Harry to the left. The directions are significant, if we accept a clue from Jung: the right side is masculine, "the rational, the conscious, the logical and the virile; the left representing the converse."[8] Accordingly, Harry must explore still further the female world of the anima, while Hermine acquaints herself with the masculine self that Harry dimly reflects. At the end of the tour she finds two men: Pablo the lover and Harry the killer. At the end of his, he finds her. Prepared by the "pleasant dance, the treatise . . ., and the little stimulant" (pp. 176-177), Harry leaves the personality of the Steppenwolf and enters into the first of five of the thousand personalities of the true Self.

The pacifist Harry finds himself involved in a hilarious guerrilla war; in the causes of population control, anti-technology, and ecology, he and his friend Gustav—a wild boy become a Protestant theologian—gun down a half-dozen automobiles and their occupants, the automobiles busily engaged meanwhile running down humans. Not that it matters which side they fight on; the point is to reduce the population as swiftly as possible, clear out the machine civilization and make room for a new start. Harry would firmly agree with the goal, but the means would have repelled him. Now caught up in an exhilarating death-orgy, similar in its impact to the emotions felt in Hell, he and Gustav merrily bang away, derisively cracking jokes all the while and enjoying the fine view of the countryside in their idle moments. Harry plunges into the violence, the irrationality, and the chaos that he has repressed all his life—and has a hell of a good time in this whimsical slaughter of men and the machines which have brought an end to all that he ever valued.

Connecting this irrational world with that of Hermine is Dora, the handsome young stenographer who emerges from the wrecked automobile of Attorney-General Loering, a dying man with Hermine's sad gray eyes. There arises a debate on the merits of their actions, which introduces another theme related to Hermine—the child—and one related to the Magic Theater, madness. Harry and Gustav establish that while their acts are mad and childish, they are morally equivalent to those of the prosecutor who kills men out of duty or those of the sane, technological over-organized states which kill men's souls with standardization and routine. Society is mad and dying any way one looks at it—and Harry's way is a lot more fun. He and Gustav pause in their slaughter only when they see a naive looter rummaging through the wrecked automobiles and then pausing to enjoy a lunch in the pleasant countryside. They feel disgusted with their bloodshed when they see "a man whose behavior was harmless and peaceable and childlike and who was still in a state of innocence" (p. 189). Yet Hesse takes one final crack at the other side: "But in the war there must have been generals even who felt the same" (p. 190). They leave their sniper's nest to follow his example and have a good lunch, Harry planning to have Dora for dessert. With that healthy decision, the war vanishes. Through his first trip into the Magic Theater, Harry has immersed himself in the destructive element he has always abhorred, finds it valuable emotionally and morally, and, purged, turns to matters of higher value: innocence, peace, food and sex.

There is an interlude as Harry hunts for another attractive room. On the way, he sees eight signs: MUTABOR promises to lead Harry beyond the souls of men to the souls of animals and plants, selves underlying the human personality. KAMASUTRAM entices him with a beginner's course in sex positions—merely forty-two, for the possibilities of mankind are infinite! DELIGHTFUL SUICIDE suggests destroying the wretched ego by laughing it "to bits" like the fragments of Harrys that popped out of the gigantic mirror. WISDOM OF THE EAST promises the route to pure spirituality while DOWNFALL OF THE WEST tempts Harry with a magnificent sequel to the Great Automobile Hunt. COMPENDIUM OF ART teaches the route through music into a timeless eternity in space. LAUGHING TEARS will synthesize the tragedy.and comedy of Harry's life into an emotion beyond and yet including each. SOLITUDE MADE EASY will instruct him to find the exhilarating society which he now sees in the Self, in exchange for the boring one of the ego.

Harry moves from the chaos of the Great Automobile Hunt to the unity of the Personality Chess game. Personality chess is not only the operation of the Magic Theater in small but looks back to the manifold selves of the completed Siddhartha and forward to the Bead Game of *Magister Ludi.* Its importance is suggested by reference to it in the final paragraph of *Steppenwolf.* In opposition to scientific theory, it argues that unity and infinite variety are not contradictory. One has so many "pieces" (the thousand souls of the gigantic mirror), each of which has the same origin and exists within the single Self. But, as in an actual chess game, the combinations of moves are infinite, so the possibilities of new personalities are infinite. Yet all belong "to the same world and acknowledged a common origin. Yet each was entirely new" (p. 193). This "art of life" is accessible to the "madman," who realizes the vast possibilities of being within the Soul and would be committed to an asylum by the one-dimensional men of science. The route to him is through the "art and . . . fantasy" of the two-dimensional man, Harry Haller and presumably the novelist Hesse. In the next two episodes, Harry will experience first the duality of the Steppenwolf and then the marvelous multiplicity of the "madman."

After two entertaining and edifying experiences, Harry has a horrifying one. In contrast to the comedy of one-dimensional victims in the Great Automobile Hunt is the diabolic destruction of one's self, the cardinal sin from which comes the holocaust of the Hunt. Harry re-experiences, now from the outside, the process of his personality. Eased by the Great Automobile Hunt and illuminated by Personality Chess, Harry learns to see the wolf as something other than the principle of static evil in his personality. Harry can now see his primitive, instinctual nature as "large, beautiful . . . noble." The wolf has "learned to belie his nature." Whipped on by the pompous animal-tamer who has "a malicious and decidedly unpleasant resemblance" to Harry, the fine animal has become a starved, cowering, submissive performing dog (pp. 194-5). Its nature is so perverted that it eats chocolate instead of meat. But the ego's vicious repression of the animal rebounds on itself; the wolf-tamer must in turn give control to the wolf, for though there is submission, there cannot be elimination without destroying life itself. Now the man becomes an "animal" under the wolf's control, snarling at the love of a beautiful girl, as has Harry, and slaughtering a lamb and a rabbit, chewing their flesh and drinking their blood. In horror and fear, his mouth tasting of blood and chocolate, Harry flees. Faced with this deepest and most terrible destruction of humanity, a foul perversion of the best in both of his natures, he sees even the traumatizing horrors of World War I as humane in comparison to what he has done to one human being—himself:

> Today I knew that no tamer of beasts, no general, no insane person could hatch a thought or a picture in his brain that I could not match myself with one every bit as frightful, every bit as savage and wicked, as crude and stupid (p. 196).

Harry has realized that the part of himself he had thought most noble and civilized was in fact his basest part. It is the seed of war and human brutality.

Peace made with the wolf, Harry feeds it in the next booth, where he makes love to all of the women he had ever frightened away. He experiences the fullest range of love from the most magnificent to that which is "unimaginable, frightful, deadly" (p. 202).

Written in a highly sensual and ecstatic style, much of this episode is about Harry's first love, Rosa Kreisler, with whom he identified Hermine. This love he now experiences with the full passion of the teenage male. Through this erotic episode, he merges also into the beauty of all nature, the nature of his animal being merging in ecstasy with the river, the spring wind, the taste of a leaf in his mouth. Filled with the "dread pleasure and pain of spring," he sees the girl "with the whole deadly foreboding of love, the foreboding of woman," and experiences in love the "enormous possibilities and promises, nameless delight, unthinkable bewilderments, anguish, suffering, release to the innermost and deepest guilt" (p. 198). When he had met her in his former life, he stood silent and let her pass. Now freed by the Magic Theater, he tells her of his love, she responds, and through the ensuing days, step by step they enter into their love affair. Hundreds of such episodes follow, involving all of the women that had been, could be, and will be. At the end of "the unending stream of allurement and vice and entanglement,"

> I was calm and silent. I was equipped, far gone in knowledge, wise, expert—ripe for Hermine. She rose as the last figure in my populous mythology, the last name of an endless series; and at once I came to myself and made an end of this fairy tale of love; for I did not wish to meet her in this twilight of a magic mirror. I belonged to her not just as this one piece in my game of chess—I belonged to her wholly. Oh, I would

now so lay out the pieces in my game that all was centered in her and led to fulfillment (p. 203).

The left side of the Magic Theater has equipped Harry for the marriage for which Hell had provided the nuptial dance. In the Automobile Hunt he has seen the value and humor of the irrational, the higher value of innocence; in the Taming of the Steppenwolf he has seen the value and necessity of maintaining harmony between man and his instincts; in the last episode he has seen the beautiful rewards of experiencing his being as natural man and has come to know woman and love her without reservation, and he has gained foreknowledge there of the Chessgame's promise of infinite variety and beauty of the whole man. But, as he turns to seek Hermine so that he can experience with her the promises he has intuited, Harry sees the last sign. He shudders as he reads: HOW ONE KILLS FOR LOVE.

Harry has left the world of Eros, having intuited the quality of immortality: ecstatic harmony with nature and humanity. But, at the moment he feels such completion, he denies the world that gave it to him: the Magic Theater is a "fairy tale." The ego denies the reality of that which it does not comprehend and strips itself of that which nourished it. For Harry, Hermine is reality—he "belonged to her wholly" (p. 203). Here is a second error, seed of the first. Harry is mistaking the part for the whole, the anima for the Self. In relieving himself of his anxieties about women, Harry thinks he has scaled the highest peak, but he has merely reached the foothills. The fool turns from the trip to the inner Self, the very seat of human reality, to the outside world of mere physical fact.

Instantly, warnings clang. Death grips him. Automatically, Harry responds to the "call of fate"—the fate of man who must learn error by experience. Forgetting his rejection of the Magic Theater as a fairy tale, he clutches at the pieces which he carried from the Personality Chessgame—he will rearrange his being—but they have become a knife. He has fallen. The gigantic mirror appears again. He sees only the wolf, ambiguously beautiful and brutal. Pablo, Hermine, and the chessmaster are gone. He looks into the mirror once more. He has diminished even further; there is only the ego there: "It was I." The old Harry faces him, weary and gray from the assaults upon its conception of itself as Self. It is "waiting for death" (p. 204); the chessmen can no longer help him. He can find release only through the knife.

At this moment, the Self reappears to guide Harry, in the only guise that Harry can respond to. Mozart appears —Mozart, from whose music Harry had first sensed immortality, though he has not seen that immortality was within himself. His "death" translates itself into romantic literary terms, suitable for the consumption of the refined intellect. Leaving the self-mutilation of the wolf in him to embark upon an equally terrible brutality in the name of love, Harry, the foolish Don Juan sees himself as Mozart's Don Giovanni just before the statue of a man he has murdered is about to take him off to Hell; Harry has tried to deny Self, which now in its permanent, undying form (the stone) will patiently run him through the ordeal again and again until he recognizes It. Within the terrible music there is laughter.

With Mozart suddenly in his presence, Harry forgets the Theater, death and Hermine; he becomes slavish in his eagerness to have his intellectual pretensions ratified by the Master, who is Ego perfected into godhood in Harry's erroneous opinion. But, whereas Pablo spoke like Mozart at the beginning of the Magic Theater, Mozart disappointingly now speaks like Pablo. Mozart is unimpressed by Harry's excited barrage of musical criticism, for he has "given up the trade" (p. 205). Then Mozart shows his new Don Juan the real Hell. As symbolized by Brahms and Wagner and then Harry's (Hesse's) own literary efforts, it is the punishment of the "superfluous." Every human act which does not lead to the realization of the Self becomes an additional barrier between the ego and the Self. The greatest human achievement is nothing if it does not lead the human, and humanity, to the Self, to the "personal." And thus a "great" man will become as irrelevant to mankind as Hesse feels that Brahms, Wagner, and he himself will be, unless beneath the "rotten plagiarisings ill-gotten" he has managed to bungle through to the Immortal Self within us and to nurture it towards fruition (p. 207).

Enraged to see his ego-achievements disparaged—Mozart raucously insults Harry in rich eighteenth-century slang—Harry attacks his God as if he were an equal; whereupon Mozart soars up into the glacial world of the Immortals—or down into the eternal world of the Self—Harry pitifully hanging on to his pigtail and fainting in a world for which he is not prepared, despite his illusions in Eros. Still, in the last moment of consciousness, he savors the delight of a "bitter-sharp and steel-bright icy gaiety . . . and a desire to laugh as shrilly and wildly and unearthly as Mozart had done" (p. 208). The moment before he commits a "tragic" act, he senses the grand comedy of the true universe of the whole man.

Gaining consciousness, Harry finds himself once more before the great mirror of the psyche, looking "much the same as on that night when he visited the professor and sat through the dance at the Black Eagle" (p. 208). He reviews his accomplishments: his maturation, the spontaneity of the dance, the insights of the Magic Theater, the laughter of the universe. These events have led him past the fear of "dancing and women and knives." He looks again and sees in himself the boy-lover, the philosopher, the musician, the pacifist, the oriental mystic, the lonely drinker, the lover of both the ideal and the sensual woman, and the man of the Magic Theater: anarchist, sexual athlete, acquaintance of the Immortals. His effort has been heroic; he has made sundry holes in the web of time and rents in reality's disguise, though it held him a prisoner still (p. 208).

But he is still "old Harry, old weary loon" (p. 209).

Bitterly, Harry shatters the mirror and turns to the Magic Theater. It is closed. He becomes again the wolf-man, knife in hand, headed for a "strange marriage." He pauses before the only unlocked door on the left side of the Theater. He moans a melancholy, romantic lament: "O Rosa! O departed youth! O Goethe! O Mozart! (p. 209). He opens the door.

There before him lie the beautiful, nude bodies of Pablo and Hermine, "side by side in a sleep of deep exhaustion after love's play" (p. 209). Emotionlessly, mechanically, Harry shoves the knife into the love-bite beneath Hermine's left breast. She opens her eyes "in wonder" and dies. Pablo awakens, smiles at the corpse, covers her left side and leaves. Harry's paralysis dissolves into a mixture of confusion, horror, and great sorrow. He has committed an act of absolute evil, greater even than his perpetual mutilation of the wolf; he has "stopped the heart of all life" (p. 210). But the coldness of Hermine's "stony brow" turns from temperature to sound—to the music of the Immortals. And Mozart re-enters.

Harry has—as he only partially suspects—done the right thing. But the act contains both good and evil. While Harry as ego had been exploring the left side of the Magic Theater (the world of the anima), Hermine had been exploring the right side of the Theater, which led her to the perfected masculine Self, to Pablo. Her dying emotion of wonder, while Pablo smiles, suggests the reintegration of the anima into the Self and the desired end of it as an independent entity. That is why her body evokes the coldness and the music of the world of the Self's eternity, beyond the space-time continuum in which the ego is trapped. Harry's act is right. In accord already with that in life which is the "deepest and

94

most beautiful, spirit, art, and thought" (p. 126), the male ego ends the rule of its female principle in response to the needs of the anima itself as well as its own.

But Harry's act is also wrong. Isolated and external not only to the anima but to the Self, the ego has not brought into consciousness the operations of its great foundation. It regards with surprise, confusion, sorrow, and horror the right movements of the total being striving to emerge. And thus, though the anima integrates with the total male Self, it does not integrate with the ego. Harry will again have to live through his problems with it.

To take the act out of the realm of the psyche into that of society, consider this possibility: what a man will do to himself, he will do to others, especially if it is true that he can react clearly to others only to the extent that he sees himself in them. Even if such repression was originally intended to honor the rights and needs of others, it won't work. The desire is merely exiled from the conscious to the unconscious where it blindly develops free from the control of the conscious to assume another guise and re-emerge in an even more destructive act. If civilization (product and in turn shaper of the conscious) demands that its individuals repress rather than integrate, it places itself in jeopardy. Civilization is altogether too young and weak to challenge a cultural unconscious that is rooted not only in man but in that which he shares with animal, plant, and, ultimately, the stone. If civilization demands the death of 999/1000 of the Self, civilization itself must die. William Blake, in *The Marriage of Heaven and Hell*, made what I once considered an unbelievably shocking statement: "Sooner murder an infant in its cradle than nurse unacted desire." Even without noting that nursing unacted desires brought murder into the heart in the first place, I can begin to see the merit of the advice: the man who doesn't kill the child today will consent to a Dachau tomorrow.

It doesn't make any difference whether or not Hermine is "real." If Harry can kill the symbol of a woman, he can kill a real woman, whether through the swift and merciful blow of the knife or the slow and brutal torture of daily hatred. The only escape from this dilemma is to realize that what he considers as opposed forces are, despite their opposition, part of the Whole, a single field. The "conflict" is a necessary and healthy tension between the widely differing potentialities of man's total being. Once he sees the problem as a non-problem, he will rise above it. He will cease to take it seriously. As Alan Watts put it:

> . . . even if there is to be a battle, there must be a field of battle; when the contestants really notice this they will have a war dance instead of a war.[9]

Harry must learn to laugh.

Yet no experience is wasted. Harry's act contains grace. He feels that he has committed absolute evil by destroying what he erroneously believes to be the very foundation of life. Yet he is forgiven, released, and fortified to continue the great strife of Self-realization. Man grows only by accepting within himself all of his potential for evil as well as his potential for good. Thereby he moves beyond both to the wholeness of a god.

Mozart returns to enforce this point. But this time he is in twentieth-century clothing and holds that symbol of the technology which Harry abhors: the radio. It "murders" the music as Harry has murdered Hermine; but he doesn't see the analogy and cries out in horror at the sound of the technology of man's debased ego killing the art of its most elevated spirit. Mozart merely laughs. Technology is in the same illusory space-time continuum as is Harry's afflicted ego; the conflict between it and art is analogous to the conflict between Harry's ego and the eternal world within him striving to be realized. When Mozart makes that point, it begins to dawn on

Harry that the decision to kill Hermine was his own rather than hers. But he still doesn't see who "he" is, that "he" is not only Harry but Hermine and Pablo/Mozart. And so Harry, thinking that he has killed "another," swears that he has "no other desire than to pay and pay and pay . . . to lay my head beneath the axe and pay the penalty of annihilation" (p. 214).

Mozart mocks him. The ego's ravages upon the Self cannot be resolved by annihilation; they can only be redeemed by integration achieved through awareness of what the ego is in relation to the whole psyche. This ego's mood will lead to a real end—to physical suicide. But Mozart goes along with him. He will "kill" the ego in a different way; he will introduce it to an emotion that is alien to it, an emotion that comes only from the Self. He will introduce it to humor, a "gallows-humor" that laughs at both life and death from the viewpoint of the whole and the eternal embodied in each individual man, in mankind, and in Siddhartha's All (p. 214). Mozart takes Harry to the guillotine and "removes his head" by leading twelve men (other mysterious elements of Hesse's being) in the Cosmic Horselaugh. The "head" or ego is momentarily indulged its illusions—it *is* cut off from the rest of the personality which rejects its tragic seriousness as inharmonious with the nature of man. Harry becomes unconscious.

Harry awakens to hear Mozart condemn him as a creature dedicated to suffering and death and tragedy and he swears that Harry will learn greater courage. He threatens him with a reincarnation of Hermine, but Harry balks. Instead Mozart orders him to come to terms with the eternal in the modern technological age:

> You are to live and to learn to laugh. You are to learn to listen to the cursed radio music of life and to reverence the spirit behind it and to laugh at its distortions. So there you are. More will not be asked of you (p. 216).

Forgetting Mozart's power, Harry rebels. But Mozart offers him another of his "charming cigarettes" (p. 217), whereupon Mozart becomes Pablo, who in turn Harry now recognizes as the Personality Chessmaster. Harry regains the sense of the possibilities that he had had in the Magic Theater; the knife has become the chessmen once more. Pablo becomes gigantic as the once-important Hermine shrinks to a "toy figure," Goethe's toy scorpion, for the all-important, all-consuming love which absorbed the ego is a mere toy of the Self to entice that ego to recognize it and give its vast dimensions conscious realization, just as is the cigarette which opened the Self to Harry in the Magic Theater.

At the very end of the novel, Harry momentarily understands all. He sees that Pablo is Mozart embodied in the twentieth century. He will inspire Harry to play the chessgame again—and again and again:

> A glimpse of its meaning had stirred my reason and I was determined to begin the game afresh. I would sample its tortures once more and shudder again at its senselessness. I would traverse not once more, but often, the hell of my inner being (pp. 217-218).

Still largely blinded by the ego's vision of the world, Harry will suffer tragedy, torture, senselessness, and hell. He has far to go to gain the humor of the immortal Self. Yet he will strive to reach that Self through seeking it in that which is about him, in his age, in Pablo. And then he will join the Mozart that he has always yearned towards:

> One day I would learn how to laugh. Pablo was waiting for me, and Mozart too (p. 218).

But if Harry hasn't learned how to laugh yet, Hesse has. Through this novel, he has attained much more firmly the vision of comedy than has the ego-bound, tragic

Harry. For Hesse not only suffers with Harry; he also laughs at him and with him, gracefully and charmingly through the being of Hermine, magnificently through Mozart. A Harry might die. A Hesse will not.

CHAPTER THREE

Narcissus and Goldmund:

The World of the Mother

Narcissus and Goldmund presents the universe as dual—
"male" and "female"—and, like *Steppenwolf* (which Hesse
finished not long before), explores the female side ex-
tensively.[1] The "world of the mother" not only refers to
the many women and sexual relationships prominent in
this novel but to all that we mean when we use the
term "Nature." It encompasses the instinctive and the
primitive, the unconscious and its dreams and fantasies,
the whole material world and its transient cycles of birth
and death. The mystery of death and its paradoxically

beautiful aspects particularly concern Hesse. In contrast to the mother-world is that of the "father": the rational and the civilized, the conscious, the permanent world of the immortal spirit. Although the father-world of Narcissus receives considerable attention here and will become dominant in *Magister Ludi,* its main function in this novel is to clarify by contrast the mother-world of Goldmund.

An even more important subject in *Narcissus and Goldmund* is the nature and function of the artist. Hesse will conclude that the artist derives from the mother-world, can transcend it through his art to attain achievements equal to those of the father-world, but must finally succumb to it. The artist's death, however, is a *completion,* rather than an end.

As always, Hesse's most important concern in *Narcissus and Goldmund* is realization of the Self and therefore synthesis of the two worlds. Harry Haller has vowed to "traverse not once more, but often, the hell of my inner being" (p. 218). Goldmund is one of the thousand souls of Hermann Hesse, and a very important one for him to explore.

For all its perplexing concerns, *Narcissus and Goldmund* can be enjoyed as a medieval romance, as indicated by its great success among its first German readers, who had deplored the shocking incidents and puzzling experimentalism of *Steppenwolf.*[2] In a series of conversations between the two protagonists, one main issue of the novel is spelled out: the relative values of the world of the ascetic intellectual (Narcissus) and the sensual artist (Goldmund). The central section—over half the novel—dramatically presents the erotic and violent adventures of Goldmund. There is, in short, plenty to satisfy either the intellectual or the sensualist.

Like *Siddhartha* and *Steppenwolf, Narcissus and Goldmund* has a basic three-part structure: it begins in a world dominated by the intellectual, enters into the rehabilitating world of the sensualist, and re-emerges—in the final conversations of the two main characters—in an integration of the two world views. Instead of Siddhartha's mystical self-immersion or Haller's humor, the integrating element is now art.

As in the other two novels, there is a subterranean emphasis that gives *Narcissus and Goldmund* a special character. In all three books, that emphasis finally emerges in a concluding puzzle that doesn't seem to be explained by Hesse's explicit statements or through character conversations. In *Siddhartha*, the puzzle appears in the parable of the stone and Govinda's vision of Siddhartha; the reader is left hanging unless he works back through the undertones of the novel. In *Steppenwolf*, the puzzle is even more evident; the reader loses the last third of the novel unless he comes to terms with the unexplained realities of Hesse's world. But in *Narcissus and Goldmund*, the puzzle is not quite so evident; perhaps the reception of *Steppenwolf* discouraged Hesse from relying so heavily on the method of presenting through dream symbol a more direct experience of psychic reality than could Jung's abstractions. In this novel, the reader can safely pass over Goldmund's infrequent dreams. But he cannot help being stopped by Goldmund's last, enigmatic words:

> But how will you die when your time comes, Narcissus, since you have no mother? Without a mother, one cannot love. Without a mother, one cannot die (p. 311).

Why cannot one die without a mother? A reader could skip over this final, briefly-stated puzzle and still feel that the novel had brought much in entertainment and intellectual insight. But if he pauses, he will be driven back through all the other minor mysteries of the book, return through the apparently simple adventures of Goldmund and see their intimate relationship with the initial and concluding conversations, recognize the importance of the references to the worlds of the father and the mother in those conversations, see the intimate connection and progression that exists between this novel and those preceding it, and discover finally the impressive depths of Hesse's probing the human psyche through the apparently clear and comprehensible medium of this "simple" medieval romance. We must attend closely to the inobtrusive network of symbols through which Hesse presents his main reactions to the mother-world, for the symbol is the expressive mode of the mother. These have been present in *Siddhartha and Steppenwolf* too. Now, freed from the necessity of commenting upon oriental theology and Jungian theory, I can pay greater attention to them. I *must* do so, for this novel forces me to as the other two did not.

The first six chapters of *Narcissus and Goldmund*, covering a three-year period, are set in a late-medieval monastery, Mariabronn. In these chapters Hesse develops a contrast between the father-world of Narcissus and the mother-world of Goldmund. The point of view is first that of a distant narrator telling an ancient legend. Quickly, it becomes distributed among the first characters, the saintly and similarly objective Abbot Daniel, the simple Father Anselm, the ascetic and brilliant Narcissus, and with increasing intensity the turbulent mind of Goldmund, who is torn between the paternal world of the monastery and the maternal world of nature within and outside him. His conflicts, his natural inclination toward the mother-world, the philosophical and psychoanalytical insights of Narcissus (a medieval Jung) and the sexual attractions of a braided servant girl and the peasant's wife Lise combine to force his departure from Mariabronn to follow his true nature.

Through the next ten chapters (and ten years) that search leads Goldmund through a series of adventures in the countryside and towns. His experiences produce in him an intimate awareness of the natures of love, death, and art. These episodes are among the most compelling in Hesse's work. They are crowded with briefly- but well-drawn characters, many of them women: the farmer Kuno and his wife; Lydia and Julie, the mutually jealous virginal daughters of a knight; a woman giving birth and the peasant Christine; Lisbeth, the daughter of the famous woodcarver, Meister Niklaus; the crippled servant girl, Marie; Goldmund's companions during the period of the Black Plague, the coward Robert and the domestic Lene; Rebekka, the Jewess, deranged by the pogrom in which her father was slaughtered; and finally the magnificent Agnes, the most complete and challenging woman of Goldmund's life, the woman who brings him to his death. Throughout these episodes, Goldmund learns the nature of woman and, from the two murders he commits as well as from the plague, the nature of death. He comes to realize the intimate relationships between death and life and the world of the woman. Finally, due to his growth as an artist under Meister Niklaus, he comes to see the possibility of uniting and transcending life and death through the artist's embodiment of the universal in man.

This integration occurs in the last four chapters (covering three years) of the novel. There the exhausted and defeated Goldmund receives treatment from Narcissus, now the Abbot of Mariabronn. As Goldmund begins to carve for the monastery, Narcissus leads him into a fuller realization of the implications of his adventures, while Narcissus himself comes to realize the proximity of the world of the artist to his own. More important, the ascetic Narcissus learns to love. But Goldmund, after completing his second project, returns for another meeting with Agnes. It kills him. Dying the beautiful death of a saint, Goldmund asks his final question of his friend: "But how will you die when your time comes, Narcissus, since you have no mother" (p. 311)?

The world of the father is that principle of the psyche which embodies intelligence, reason, the faculties of analysis, logic, organization, and control. Its symbols in this novel are often light and desert. But the presentation of the father-world isn't frequently symbolized, a fact that may lead a reader to underemphasize its importance in the book; Narcissus is able to *state* his case quickly and precisely in a series of conversations beginning and ending the novel. This is the mode of the expository writer: emotionless, objective, static, abstract. He stands in one position, thinks much, acts little. He is the unmoving mind watching and interpreting events. He uses the word. But Goldmund's existence—an existence closer to instinct, sensation, and, through its female orientation, the unconscious and the inexpressible whole Self—is one which Hesse must create through the suggestion of symbol and the moving drama of symbolic event and character.

Narcissus is the radical father who has stringently repressed the feminine qualities of the male personality. His is the "service of the mind . . . the word" which Siddhartha turns his back upon. He leads his students toward "high spiritual goals" (p. 17). He lives in the conscious mind, repressing his human responses to his students, repressing the erotic sensations he feels in the presence of the beautiful Goldmund; and this eroticism can only be that of male to male, for the deepest repression is of the mother's world and all that it represents. Narcissus is a "scientist," a man who analyzes, establishes the differences between men, recognizes their individuality; such fragmentation leads to understanding but not to the wholeness of life. As Narcissus puts it:

> . . . we creatures of reason, we don't live fully; we live in an arid land, even though we often seem to guide and rule . . . . ours is the world of ideas . . . . ours is the danger of suffocating in an airless void. I am a thinker . . . . I wake in the desert (p. 43).

Hesse's points are so far pretty clear. But there are some aspects of Narcissus' character which might cause some difficulties: his intuition (a traditional feminine characteristic), his need to "serve others by ruling over them" (p. 5), and his deep attraction to his opposite, Goldmund. In discussing intuition, Hesse is probably again mindful of Jung, who believed that intuition, along with thinking, feeling, and sensation, was a basic function of *any* personality, not simply the feminine. The difference between Narcissus and Goldmund lies in the function of intuition in their different personalities. For Narcissus, its perceptions are constantly translated into the conscious as information and knowledge about others. He is very much like an expert psychoanalyst who, intuiting the hidden operations of others' personalities, is able to translate these into intellectual terms to make his patients consciously aware of what they are doing and why they are doing it. Although such conscious awareness may not necessarily lead to a change of behavior (as it does when Narcissus performs this service for Goldmund), it does give the intuitive intellectual added power over the individuals about him.

This point leads to the next problem—service by rule. Narcissus' intuition about himself, implicit in his name, is that his greatest danger is "pride," exaltation of his conscious, thinking self over all other functions—and all other people. Such narcissistic self-absorption leads to destruction of the total Self and, accordingly, to destruction of others. Unable to relate to others directly and intimately through the functions of feeling and sensation, Narcissus must control his self-destructive power by putting it in the service of others, by ruling them as he sees they must be ruled in order to obtain for themselves their own self-realization. This act he performs for Goldmund, thereby liberating a man who stands for all that he himself is not.

Both points explain his attraction for Goldmund. Even more important than the father-world to Narcissus is the world of the self-realizing person. He clearly sees that his highest duty and that of others is self-realization. It makes no difference that heredity and environment have set for Goldmund entirely different terms than they have for him: the goal is to become who you are, no matter who you are—it is the highest morality. Goldmund attracts him because the boy is one of the "unconditioned "described in *Steppenwolf*'s "Treatise," one of that group of "saints and sinners" (Narcissus being the saint, Goldmund the sinner) whose fate it is to be impelled past the one-dimensional self of the middle class into an intense search for the real Self, despite the pain and horror of the process. Narcissus and Goldmund are, despite their vast differences, identical in the most important sense: they seek in their lives the immortal Self, each in his own way.

I have over-emphasized the father-world of Narcissus to the point of obliterating Hesse's conception of him as a human. Hesse spends much time obliquely giving substance to this abstracted man. He is extremely handsome, dark, straight, and slender. Most prominent are his eyes and mouth. The eyes are quiet but piercing, "cool, sparkling." The voice is also "cool, controlled, matter-of-fact, . . . compelling . . . inspired, untiring" (p. 11); the lips are "beautiful, sharply outlined" (p. 3). He is a charismatic teacher, commanding respect and obedience. In his manner, he is grave, aristocratic, noble, refined. For all his power and control, he is dangerously attracted to the beautiful Narcissus, both spiritually and physically. There is tense, suppressed drama in his struggle to overcome the compulsion of his body and emotions so that he can guide the boy to the path he must take. This selfless act performed, there remains the quiet but powerful dramatization of the terrible nature of Narcissus' course as he withdraws to his cell where his wasting body mirrors the dynamic conflicts within him. Underlying all is his tragic awareness that someday he will need Goldmund to complete him by insights that he will never be able to obtain. Goldmund does so at the end of the novel in words that will burn "like fire in his heart" (p. 312). The commitment to the world of the father is no easier a route than that to the world of the mother.

And yet that commitment, because of Goldmund's existence, is eventually not a full one. Compelled by a sensual and physical love for the boy, Narcissus learns to integrate the ability to love in his own personality; it lies not in succumbing to homosexuality, which would destroy the very foundation of his personality, but in elevating it to a spiritual plane through a self-abnegating service to Goldmund. That service is to free him to find his own way. And, in performing that act, an act of pure love, Narcissus begins to learn something from the world of the mother, the necessity of the "language of the soul" taught him by Goldmund's example of imaginative power; it is the only way in which he can understand and reach the boy—reason and words are not enough. But all that the unrealized Goldmund can now provide him is the intuition of the nature of this other valid route to God. Goldmund must go out into the world and find his nature as fully as has Narcissus before he can return to the monastery and bring Narcissus closer to completion.

But in this novel, Hesse is chiefly concerned with the exploration of one of the most immediately compelling routes to Self in his own personality, the route through Goldmund's mother-world, which he must follow to its end before he can "die" and be reborn into the much different personality of the Magister Ludi. Through Goldmund, Hesse creates a powerful work, realizing his experience not only through the wood-carver's adventures and through his sensuous experience of nature but, most important, through the oblique and mysterious technique of the dream and the symbol. Like Hermine, Goldmund is in close contact with the world of the unconscious and is able to bypass the abstract word for the concrete, meaningful image. When they do not appear in his fantastic and puzzling dreams, these symbols are worked inobtrusively into the texture of the novel, as is the powerful symbol of the chestnut tree. It is easy to pass over them as mere description. Although it is better that a reader allow the symbols to work on him, as they may lead to personal insights, I will discuss some of the more important ones as I trace Goldmund's career. But Hesse does not rely on symbols exclusively. He provides amply for the conscious mind by plot, character, and explicit commentary. The last element so pervades the novel that some readers complain that Hesse leaves nothing unexplained. I would put it a little differently: he leaves nothing unexplained that *can be* explained.

Toward the end of the novel, Goldmund has an insight about the progression of his life:

> It seemed to Goldmund that his life had been given a meaning. For a moment it was as though he were looking down on it from above, clearly seeing its three big steps: his dependence on Narcissus and his awakening; then the period of freedom and wandering; and now the return, the reflection, the beginning of maturity and harvest (p. 270).

During the first stage of Goldmund's progression, the awakening, Narcissus manages to bring to the surface several facts about Goldmund's childhood. Goldmund was the son of totally incompatible parents. His father was a nobleman of political importance. His mother was a beautiful noblewoman but one who had been born poor and left uneducated in Christianity—a "natural woman," a pagan. Although her husband tried to educate her, she rebelled, slept with other men, and earned a local reputation as a witch. Finally, she deserted both husband and son to follow the dictates of her self. Although as a child Goldmund had loved her very much, his bitter father forced him to repress that love and regard his mother as evil. Reminded continually of his wife by the boy, who looked exactly like her, the father finally freed himself forever by leaving Goldmund at a monastery where he was to live a monk's life in expiation for the sins of his mother.

At the beginning of the novel, Goldmund is a vital,

handsome, sensitive boy whose total being denies his conscious determination to become an ascetic. He seeks love—and is torn violently by his attraction to the contrasting natures of the saintly, human Abbot Daniel and the cold intellectual Narcissus. When he is first kissed by a young girl, Goldmund is traumatized; all that he has denied in himself now assaults the conscious image of himself imposed by his father. Narcissus then becomes Goldmund's friend; he has long recognized in the boy a nature opposite to his own. Now Goldmund's distress overcomes Narcissus' fear of becoming too sensually involved with him and the ascetic begins to probe, much like a modern psychoanalyst, into the boy's psyche. He learns of the traumatizing incident with the girl, and this discovery leads him to an intuition of the existence of a deeper repression. Narcissus virtually bungles onto the truth during a somewhat pontifical and rhetorical analysis of the differences between their characters, differences which Goldmund has denied and is so deeply distressed at hearing that he flees and eventually sinks into a coma. While in this state, Goldmund has a beautiful dream of his mother which restores her image to him in all its power and beauty. He awakens healed.

Goldmund now enters a period of sensuality and of dreaming, during which he gradually recognizes and accepts the differences between himself and his friend, who is turning from him to follow a spiritual course. Goldmund decides that he must leave the monastery and never return to his father. Then Goldmund falls in love; he is seduced by a gypsy, Lise. He returns to the monastery to part with Narcissus in friendship and turns his back upon Mariabronn to enter the world to follow, like his mother, the dictates of his self.

Through Narcissus' statements, Hesse makes it partially clear what Goldmund's true self is. It consists of three elements. Most important, because the most universally significant, is that Goldmund is one of the "unconditioned," a special human being destined to take the difficult path of self-realization. Second, his greatest ability will be to fall in love easily and quickly and to give himself fully—whether to life or death. Third, Goldmund's ultimate approach to the realm of the self will be the artist's; his originality will fuse in him a dangerous sensuality with a redeeming spirituality.

To realize himself as lover and artist, Goldmund must enter the mother-world. It is the world of the child and the vital youth, of beauty, dreams and the dreaming artist, of sexuality and perceptive sensual response to human and natural realities. To live in the mother-world is to live in nature rather than in heaven; it demands a man who is both strong enough for passion and delicate enough to feel the most sensitive response, a man who has great vitality and health. Only a man like Goldmund can live in the world of the mother, of nature, of the moon.

But Narcissus' perceptions are not full, for he can see the mother-world only from the outside. The mother-world gains greater dimension if we look at it in Jungian terms and then see how Hesse, through symbolism, creates and amplifies this mother-world through Goldmund's sensory perceptions and dreams. Perhaps the trite expression, "Mother Nature," best names the mother-world. Everything that might be conventionally associated with nature or the natural belongs to the mother-world: the cycles of birth, maturity, decay and death of all living things; the associated functions of fertility, fruition, vitality, deterioration; the primitive man or the child living close to the unconscious, the instinctive and the basic drives; the intuitive and the impulsive and the imaginative; all that gives birth to the mysterious world of the dream, fantasy, and magic. It is a world that thrives without control; it is best lived in by being passively responsive to its laws.

In Hesse's view, every good has its evil. If there is birth, there must be death: nature displays cruel indifference to all suffering as it moves through cyclical processes that so often seem alien and inconsistent. Nature seen only in this aspect appears monstrous, vengeful, the enemy of life, the female monster Medusa, Lilith the enemy of Eve and birth, Kali the goddess devouring sacrificed human beings.

Between the world of the mother and the world of the father, as seen by the primitive and the child within all of us, exist many contrasts: hers is the world of matter and nature, his the disembodied spirit joining God; hers the cycles of life and death, his immortality; hers the transient, his the permanent; hers the unconscious, his the conscious intellect; hers the primitive, his the civilized.

As both Narcissus and Goldmund realize, there are many ways to the mystic center, as many ways as there are beings. But there is only one true guide, the Self. One must follow it through horror and ecstasy, good and evil, life and death. It will lead the individual back from his mutilated, fragmented state, back from the ravages of the accidental and the chaotic. A Narcissus must follow thought to the point leading him beyond itself to the Universal Self, which he now thinks of as God the Father. A Goldmund must plunge into life, its blood and semen, to the point leading him too beyond itself to the Universal Self which he now thinks of as Mother Earth. But neither Father nor Mother is an end. Beyond them is that Self which is all, that always has been there, everywhere like Siddhartha's stone, the beginning and ending of all inorganic matter. The Way is open to us all. Goldmund and Narcissus differ from the rest of us only in that they become awakened to the Way.[3] Goldmund's awareness, however, is not as clear to the conscious mind as Narcissus'. And so Hesse must present it to us through the mode of the mother, the dream from the unconscious, the image in nature that holds symbolic significance beyond itself.

Goldmund perceives this mother-world through symbol: the dream from the unconscious, the image or event in nature that has significance beyond itself. Hesse rarely introduces a landscape or lingers upon a character without having in mind the bearing that an image or event has upon the mother-world, the father-world, or the Self.

I would like to demonstrate the point by applying Cirlot's *Dictionary of Symbols* to key episodes and details in Goldmund's awakening: his night escapade with Adolf, Konrad, and Eberhard; his dream of his mother; and Mariabronn's chestnut tree and spring.

In the night escapade, the boys' names are important. *Goldmund* translates from the German as *golden mouth*, which some Hesse scholars have associated with St. John Chrysostom, an eloquent fourth century priest; indeed, the novel itself makes the identification. Although the association works insofar as Chrysostom was strongly influenced by his mother and was a man who made an art out of his speech, his ascetic life and perpetual attacks on vice don't correspond very well to Goldmund's character. I think it is more likely that Hesse, like Jung, was aware of the fiery mouth appearing in the Old Testament and, perhaps, the hieroglyph of a blue-eyed man (Goldmund's eyes are blue) with a golden disk in his mouth (the sun). The mouth is at times a symbol of creative power, its gold symbolizing divine intelligence buried in the earth; Goldmund will find the immortal Self buried in nature and reclaim it by art. But the fire of the sun and the eating mouth also destroy. Thus death also becomes associated with Goldmund's creative exhuming of the Self. And, of course, Goldmund becomes as fully acquainted with death as he does with life: death becomes an act of completion, perfection.

In the episode under analysis, the other boys' names are much simpler symbolically: *Konrad, Eberhard,* and *Adolf* mean, respectively, *bold counsellor, boar,* and *wolf.* The wolf symbolizes the instinctual seen as evil while the boar is licentiousness. To conclude, the creative realizer of the Self first enters the mother world in a spirit of boldness motivated by instincts which he himself sees as evil, which in turn are empowered by licentiousness. As in *Steppenwolf,* it is wise to regard each character as an aspect of Hesse's psyche. In actual fact, there was an episode something like this one in Hesse's youth; its memory was to remain with him for many years.[4]

The night journey through the forest and the village to the house of the girls is laden with symbols of the mother-world. The excursion through the black, damp forest and the crossing of a stream symbolizes not only a journey into the fertile world of the female but also one into the unconscious and into death (presently the death of Goldmund's father-self but ultimately the death that pervades the novel). The damp stars hidden by clouds suggest disintegration (again of the father-self) and a destiny yet obscured. Through the village, the house, the wood out of which both are made, and the garden, the mother-world appears in a different aspect: there is now control of the primeval forces of the night journey but the control is on feminine terms: that female control is emphasized by the entry through a window, both a female sexual symbol and one which, through its squareness, suggests conscious control. The control definitely isn't male, for the father-symbol of the lamp is one which dimly flickers, an image indicating that the intellect is barely functioning.

The actual encounter between the boys and girls is not only emphasized by erotic symbols but broadened into a symbolic sexual union. The boys offer a half-loaf of bread (the sexual—but only in part), incense (emotion), and candles (the individual life, here given to the female). In turn, the girls offer apple cider (earthly desires in an intoxicating form). Through these gifts, any significant element of the father-world is sacrificed or extinguished—the game belongs to the girls. All is reminiscent of a Dionysian orgy, where the male through alcohol or drugs would sacrifice consciousness (and sometimes life itself) to become in tune with the natural world dominated by the female priestesses.

While the three boys and the servant girl might indicate what subterranean elements of Hesse's personality were activated, Goldmund remains the most distinctive feature of the psyche at that moment—the father-shaped consciousness terribly threatened by an intuitive awareness of its mother-nature. He is paralyzed and will respond only to the mother in the form of the child-virgin, the quiet girl with the black braids. But even here, he is not safe: her hair while connected to the spiritual through the head and control through the braiding is also an ambiguously powerful sexual symbol; its blackness is reminiscent of the mysterious night outside. Not only are her fascinating eyes also dark, but the eye itself —a continual object of interest to Goldmund—is a symbol of the mother and the child, the iris (the mother) surrounding the pupil (the child). And of course she kisses him on the way out, an act which has erotic impact upon the virginal boy.

But in this episode Hesse has not only conveyed the mother-world symbolically and the erotic path to it through the unconscious, he has also presented the goal: the arrival at Self, at the mystic center where the forces of male and female join and balance, where humanity becomes whole and indistinguishable from the cosmos. The kiss, involving mouths, connects with the creative aspect of Goldmund's name. The kiss, the pupil of the eye, and the girl herself are all associated with the child: the child is a symbol of the whole Self, the seed of it within us striving for realization in the completed Self which has returned to the mystic center where it once began. The cider-vessel ornamented with a blue flower is of central significance: the vessel and its beverage not only symbolize the mother-world containing intoxicating desire but the area within which male and female forces intermingle. The blue flower symbolizes that in which the intermingling culminates, for it is a symbol of the mystic center, the absolute truth of the universe, the point where male and female merge in realized Self and Self merges with the cosmos in the eternal moment.

During his hasty exit, Goldmund tears his hand on a rose-bush and, as he flees, smells water, earth, and dung. The rose is not only a common symbol of the erotic passion which here has "wounded" Goldmund; as does the blue flower, it also carries the suggestion of the mystic center which he will have to "die" into through the cycles of the thousand selves. The return to water and earth signify a return to the unconscious after this moment in the psyche where mother world leads to mystic center. The smell of dung, often associated with gold and precious gems, serves as a reminder that the journey to the highest spiritual elements must lead, as it did with Harry Haller, through the lowest and most repulsive—man must accept himself totally to become his Self.

Having perhaps made the clear mysterious, let me now make the mysterious clear: Goldmund's healing dream. Its symbolic significance meshes neatly with the subjects I have just dwelled upon, subjects which permeate the whole novel, both explicitly and symbolically. Narcissus has shocked Goldmund by making him recall his forgotten mother, and Goldmund has fallen into a trance, during which he has a curative dream, out of which he awakens into a new life. The dream has two elements: (1) the three dogs' heads which he had seen on an arch just before the dream; (2) the blonde, blue-eyed mother telling him that he has forgotten his childhood. The three dogs' heads, like those of Cerberus, the three-headed dog guarding Hell, introduce not only death but the rotting in Goldmund of the three great principles of life: preservation, reproduction, and spiritual evolution becoming degraded into the desire to possess property or power, into sexual lust, and into vanity. The mother's visit is preceded by the scent of roses, combining again the mystic center with the erotic, the passionate, and the emotional. The beautiful mother, of course, introduces the mother-world. But it is no longer dark, mysterious, evocative of death. She is, like him, blonde and blue-eyed; she is associated with the sun-world of the father as well as with the beauty of the creative act. She reminds him of childhood, the unrealized Self within him, the archetypal mystic center. He awakens filled with joy and with love, the emotion to which he will become most committed. But in this moment of awakening and beginning, he sees his mother only as an alternative to the "dogs' death," not as she

116

was in the trip with the boys and will be hereafter—the symbol of a right death, a natural and necessary death Afterwards, he drinks alcohol again, but this time the wine is aromatic and sweet, restorative. The destruction of the conscious can be horrifying for anyone who holds onto it as the only way of life; but he who can transcend that conscious world into the unconscious, see it as good, and emerge again becomes tranquil and healed.

An examination of the symbol of the chestnut tree that Hesse dwells upon in the first paragraph of the novel will inevitably lead to a subject that is closely related to Goldmund's "awakening"—the integrated Self present always in Mariabronn and in its Abbot Daniel. Goldmund roams the whole world, only to find Self where he started, in Mariabronn, under the chestnut tree. Described in the sensuous prose with which Hesse often evokes the mother-world, the tree is from the south and thus grows and dies on an alien cycle, blooming in whites and greens much later than the others, reaching fruition in a "burnished gold crown" when the others are dead, nourishing the men and boys in the winter with its nuts, "secret kin" to the stone columns and ornaments of the cloister. It has died its yearly death when Goldmund returns to the monastery to die. Trees are of course common in mythologies; note our Christmas tree, associated with Mary and the birth of Christ, the "tree" upon which Christ was crucified, and the trees of Eden symbolizing Life and Knowledge. In general, the tree symbolizes through its permanence, its slow growth, and its cycles of blooming and withering, the nature of immortality and the process of growth of the individuating Self. Its roots, bole, and leaves connect the underworld, middle earth, and heaven, which further symbolizes a uniting principle in the cosmos. Bisexual in nature, the tree often appears as twin trees, male and female, life and knowl-edge—often the implicit symbolism of the two stone columns outside a monastery's entrance. Hesse's tree seems to me to belong to the world of the mother: it is from a warmer climate; it is alien to the world of the

117

father; it lives through a different cycle of birth and death; it shadows and nourishes men and boys. Yet its "gold crown" links it to the more general symbolism of the tree, such a crown signifying "the highest goal in evolution: for he who conquers himself wins the crown of eternal life."[5] And it is for the fruit of this crown that the male students "would scramble and fight" (p. 1).

Associated with the monastery is another symbol enforcing the significance of the tree as a process of masculine self-realization attained through the world of the mother. "Mariabronn" means "spring of Mary," the Great Mother of the male God who is born, dies, and is reborn. The spring is a symbol of the life-force of man, the "source of inner life and of spiritual energy"; linked with "'the land of infancy'... the need for this fount arises principally when the individual's life is inhibited and dried up."[6]

These symbols of integration can be related to one of the two men whom Goldmund loves: Abbot Daniel. This relationship may explain why the boy finds the old man such a sharp contrast to Narcissus. Abbot Daniel is cited as one of Mariabronn's three "special" men, "who seemed to be chosen" (p. 3). Although the novel has much to say about the other two, Narcissus and Goldmund, there is little space devoted to the Abbot. Yet taken in connection with the chestnut tree, the spring, and the monastery's Mary, his significance becomes clear. Abbot Daniel transcends the worlds of the two protagonists. In touch with both the masculine world of the monastery and worshipping its goddess Mary, Abbot Daniel has the deceptively simple characteristics of Siddhartha's Vasudeva. He is the man of wisdom, rather than of knowledge. He is one of Hermine's saints; he is simple, childlike, humble, gentle, patient; he has the saving grace of the Immortal— humor. Most significant, he distrusts the arrogant, rebellious intelligence of Narcissus. To Abbot Daniel, Narcissus' intellectuality is the sin of individual pride which can destroy the harmonious rhythms of the monastery. Like Goldmund, Abbot Daniel will die a good death, the death of a man in harmony with the universe rather than one of its two spheres. Abbot Daniel is the norm against which we can measure Narcissus and Goldmund, who explore the extremes of the cosmos which he encompasses in his personality, a simple one because an integrated one.

I hope that I have made the point that *Narcissus and Goldmund* is much more complex, much richer and more mysterious than it appears to be. Every episode—virtually every detail—in the novel affords the same sort of symbolic significance as the three early passages I have discussed at length. Nor is *Narcissus and Goldmund* unique in this respect; all of Hesse's major fiction contains a wealth of symbolic complexity. In *Narcissus and Goldmund*, however, Hesse has such perfect control of his symbols that he is able to work them into the novel in the simplest and most inobtrusive way. Unless the reader is truly attuned, he may skim over abysses with a sense of perfect safety. We have to follow the path of Goldmund and, like him, learn

> to puncture the skin of reality, to unleash the raging abysses, streams, and milky ways of an image world of the soul that lay beneath peacefully barren reality (p. 159).

As Harry Haller goes through numerous sexual experiences in the Magic Theater's room of love, so does Goldmund in his wandering life in countryside, castle, and city. Although this series of encounters may seem a shapeless anthology of erotic and sensational short stories, it contains a definite pattern. Hesse wishes Goldmund to experience life and death in middle-range and extremes in order to force him to the further solution of art. He submits Goldmund to three great life-death cycles. The first educates his nature through the life experiences of sensual women, the life-death transition of the virgin lover Lydia, and the death experience of Viktor. The second cycle educates his spirit through life

119

experience of the city artist and the death experience of the plague. The third distills the experiences of the other two cycles into a two-day liaison with Agnes, the first day bringing Goldmund his greatest ecstasy, the second bringing his greatest horror. He is then prepared for "autumn," the harvest of art, and for "winter," the perfect death. Although these are the main progressions, Hesse isn't this mechanical: life and death intermingle continually; spirit gleams through in the first cycle while nature suffers more in the second and third. By such intermingling, Hesse is trying to emphasize the flow and ambiguity, the variety and confusion, and the contrasts and modulations of the organic world of growth and decay of life, psyche, and society.

For the first year or two of his wandering decade, Goldmund experiences women as erotic, sensual, instinctive, physical. He learns that he is "gifted for love, for this game with women" (p. 100). Goldmund becomes sexually adroit; he learns every stimulation, every caress, every sexual position and game, each woman's way of making love. He is open and receptive, quick to inflame and compliant to every suggestion, every female fantasy. He becomes the perfect lover, attractive to "any woman with intelligent senses" (p. 99). The secret of his attraction is that which relates him to the mystic center: "his childlike openness, his inquisitive innocence" (p. 99).

But Goldmund's love relationships are like that with the gypsy, Lise. "The exalted, brief joy of love vaulted above him, burned with a golden glow, sank down and died" (p. 72). The moments of gold are brief. The transitory quality of the mother-world impresses itself upon him most; each relationship is temporary, each woman returns to where she came from, to other roles and functions. Like Lise the night he made love with her for the second time, the women Goldmund encounters are lit by the moon, ever-changing, ever-beginning and ending. In the company of some women, like Lise, he makes love within nature; he becomes harmonized with animals, plants, and trees. With others, like the wife of Kuno, he becomes acquainted with another aspect of the mother-world, the domestic. But whoever they are, the women reach out to him, find their natures reflected by him, love him—and leave him, for fathers, for husbands who beat them, for the routine of the home. Goldmund's freedom does not attract them; they must build and settle, contain within themselves the nature that responds to him. For him, the moon-like state of the sensual world becomes "this strange pain . . . this subtle fear, this grief over the transitory" (p. 96). Goldmund discovers on its least painful level the cycle of life and death, beginnings and endings, and the brevity and instability of man's moments of gold, of self-transcendence, in the mother-world. Before the novel ends, he will learn the lesson better.

Goldmund turns from the world of the complete sensualist to its radical opposite: the world of the romantic lover. The apparent inconsistencies of the episodes concerning Lydia, Julie, and Viktor can be reconciled if we consider Denis deRougemont's convincing thesis that romantic passion has as its negatives death and destruction rather than the fruition and harmony of marital love.[7] Passion is an idealizing love which demands distance from the beloved and cannot survive the intimacies of marriage. It leads to love of love itself, to the excitation of keen emotions; it seeks intoxication rather than satisfaction; it becomes a tormenting addiction; it is akin to the maddened mysticism which Narcissus feared Goldmund would embrace if he stayed within the monastery. And in fact in the world of Lydia and Julie, Goldmund does enter into a monastic existence once again and experiences as part of the world of the mother the disaster he would have encountered in the world of the father. Lise meant life to Goldmund. Lydia means death. It is the first turn of the wheel.

The Lydia episode by itself is not so puzzling. It is a familiar story retold in many a contemporary love song, film, and novel: the flirtation, the girl's jeolousy, her tantalizing of the boy, the virginal relationship carried even into the bed, where again and again she says *no* while yearning to say *yes,* her attractive whimsical girlishness, his growing tormented passivity—Goldmund can give but he can't take. The platonic passion culminates in the winter, the season of death, with the ultimate absurdity of sister Julie joining the hand-holding couple in bed and with the introduction into the old knight's household of "grief, contradiction, nonsense, alienation, and innermost confusion" (p. 122). Behind this familiar situation of passionate obsession and jealousy in a sterile setting is the shadow of Kali, the devouring goddess, although it is as the Virgin Mary that Goldmund will sculpt Lydia.

The connection between the Virgin and Kali is made by the gold piece Goldmund receives from Lydia. As the symbol of the divine intelligence and supreme illumination of the sun (to which Lydia herself is related by her gold hair and her later appearance as the Madonna), the gold coin presents that realm in the only form that the most debased of men, Viktor, can recognize it. Still in the season of winter, Goldmund kills Viktor over the gold coin, upon which each vagabond places a different value. The relationship of love and death, though still oblique, has become even clearer.

Viktor presents to Goldmund the negative side of freedom; he is the outsider who has been driven by society to survive by preying on society itself. He is the starving wolf, the scavenger, the debased priest and intellectual committed only to survival, stealing from the host, exploiting the lover, and murdering the friend. Aside from fear, Viktor's only emotion is the raucous gallows humor of the nihilistic vagabond. Goldmund learns from him the need for commitment within walls, if not the secret of the escape from isolation and transience. But the lesson brings Goldmund close to madness; once the springtime lover, he is now the winter killer stumbling in the snow and seeing death everywhere about him and deep within him. He has not yet learned what the mother will teach him: this is her season, too. Goldmund only sees winter's universality, its threat to every man, home, city, civilization. But within him, as he struggles against the death about him and the death within him, is also "this beautiful, terrifying force, this tenacity of life inside one during the last desperate struggle" (p. 139).

He emerges from the snowy wasteland into a village. The symbolic function of this village is to complete the Lydia episode and contain the Viktor episode. Between these episodes of two types of death is the brief moment in the village where Goldmund for the first time sees a woman giving birth. He relates the ecstatic pain of the woman's face to the faces of those many women he has seen in the ecstasy of orgasm, and he perceives the connection of love and birth; the experience purges him of the sterile passion he felt for Lydia: the next night he makes love to a peasant woman. Now after stumbling into the same village after killing Viktor, he makes a third link to the blend of pain and joy which he has seen in moments of love and birth: "the gestures and expressions of . . . dying" (p. 139). Birth, love, and death unify in the face and body of the person experiencing them. There is some principle beyond them. At the moment of this intuition, the seasons change and Goldmund can "hear the spring winds groan" (p. 141). Above him "the moon was changing" (p. 140). The wheel of the mother has turned again.

Goldmund begins a second cycle of life and death. His natural self was tempered by the sexuality, passion, and murders of the first; his spiritual self will become tempered by the art and plague of the second. The experience will complete him and prepare him for the synthesis of both in Agnes; in the first cycle, he found great beauty in life and, through Lydia, discovered the horror of death, its twin. Now he will live through a second period of ecstasy, see its decay, enter the world of death, and see *its* beauty.

It is the mother who first leads Goldmund into the life of the artist. And she will finally take him from it. He becomes committed to art as an alternate to his painfully transitory gypsy life when he sees the blend of pain and joy in the Madonna carved by Meister Niklaus. Goldmund intuitively realizes that the artist can transcend the mother's cycles of life and death by embodying them in a form that speaks to the eternal, static spirit of the father. In this quality, art is like the father-productions of philosophy and civilization erected against the mother's change and destruction. But art goes even farther, as Goldmund learns while using his mother talent to embody in wood the image of Narcissus, the distillation of the father:

> art was a union of the father and mother worlds,
> of mind and blood . . . was male-female, a merg-
> ing of instinct and pure spirituality (p. 169).

Unlike normal father products, art is a bridge between father and mother, not a wall; it is a marriage, not a war. Art transcends their worlds and leads most directly to the synthesized Self.

But despite its great attributes, art cannot be an end in itself. Goldmund must eventually leave it and return to the gypsy life, for he has found another set of contrasts: between the wanderer strenuously experiencing the ecstasy and horror of life, and the artist patiently, ascetically embodying that experience through his transcendent act. There is no conflict here. There is a process: the artist must enter life to gain the substance of his art, then retreat from life to transcend it in his creations, and return to it again to gain a new substance for his art.

As the work of art can create the merged mother and father, it also draws upon the worlds of both for its techniques. Meister Niklaus' personality stresses the father-mode. In Niklaus the father and the mother war; the former is the stronger. There is a strange contrast between his "lover's hands," and his "stern, already slightly graying head" (pp. 151-152). Although he can recognize the artist in Goldmund and nurture that talent, he himself is becoming sterile and aged. His head has won over his hands; he creates without inspiration now. He has sunk to the one-dimensional man, fearful, prudish, miserly; he is concerned with prestige and property; he has crippled his golden-haired daughter Lisbeth (symbol of his own denied feminine nature) by regarding her as an object to own and protect and as a tool for advancing his status.

Goldmund can submit his free spirit to the soul-stultifying routines of Niklaus *if* there is within him an image which energizes the other process of the artistic act: the mother-mode of intuition working from the unconscious to free into Niklaus' statues the image of a universal truth, a truth which will always be mysterious, though embodied, in the statue. As Goldmund becomes an artist, he sees more and more clearly what this truth might be. As he makes one kind of synthesis of nature and spirit by merging in his statue of the Apostle John the image of the Narcissus spirit shaped and purified by the intuition and love of his own feminine nature, he begins to have a vision of a greater project: the statue of Mother Eve. In his life as a wanderer, he had experienced her. Now he begins to see her. He is first led to the insight by the cyclical process of delight and melancholy in his city life; the moments of bliss with women are interpenetrated by despair in the knowledge of their imminent passing, a despair in turn interpenetrated by hope in the knowledge of a renewed moment. This present cycle extends his previous knowledge of "the intimate relationship of ecstasy to pain and death" as his new experiences with city women extends his awareness of Mother Eve's face, a face which includes all of the women he has ever known and that principle which unites them; each woman is like all others only in that she differs from all others. The mother is the principle of infinite variety in all the ranges between love, bliss, birth and cruelty, decay, death. Art brings Goldmund yet one more intuition: the face of Mother Eve will be that of a hermaphrodite. For at the point of fullest knowledge of her, he will know that she blends with the male to arrive at the Ultimate Self as does his art now synthesize the means and the images of both.

But Goldmund has only reconciled himself with Narcissus. He has not yet fully seen the face of the Mother. He must experience and accept her other aspect, death. Goldmund leaves art for the gypsy-life of his own mother. He will not be able to return to it again until he has lived further, for he has nothing left to create.

Having left art for experience, Goldmund will immerse himself in death through his encounter with the Black Plague. At the end of this ghastly episode, he will return to Meister Nicklaus, exhausted by experience, ready for the static disciplined world of the artist again, yearning for the act of creation:

> . . . figures that meant love and torture to him today, fear and passion, would stand before later generations, nameless, without history, silent symbols of human life (p. 227).

This episode is surely the most powerful and moving in the novel. In it, Hesse comes to terms with death. Like all great principles of the universe, death shares in both the worlds of father and mother. As father, it is necessary, stern, an obligation: "a warrior, a judge or hangman, a stern father" (p. 221). But, as the mother, death is

> sweet . . . and seductive, motherly, an enticement to come home . . . loving, autumnal, satiated . . . a mother and a mistress; its call was a mating call, its touch a shudder of love (p. 221).

These are the two basic points of the episode: the horror and the beauty of death, and the obligation and power of the artist to embody for mankind the mystery of his existence in order to bring meaning to a world that God has apparently deserted.

Goldmund enters the world of death with two companions, Robert and Lene, who demonstrate the limits of the male or female confronting death. Robert's failure is masculine: a spritual failure. In some ways he resembles Narcissus: homosexual in inclination, a devotee of churches, and admirer of Goldmund's mind and strength. In another sense, he is like Niklaus: a middle-class worker of wood born into the world of the security-loving. In still another sense, he is like Goldmund: a wanderer, childlike, innocent, dedicated to the transitory, instinctively surviving, rejected and hated by the city-dweller because wanderers imply the eventual death of families, homes, and cities. Yet these elements are in greater conflict in him than are the elements of male and female in Niklaus. His childishness negates his intellect; his middle-class self negates his courage. Robert is a cowardly fool. He scuttles out of the novel, totally defeated by the spiritual challenge with which death confronted him, deserting all that he had left to value or which valued him.

Lene's failure is feminine: a physical failure. She is the wife, the home-keeper, the mother. Her instinct is to serve and preserve, to build and contain, to give birth out of love. She is young, pretty, joyful, shy, inexperienced, and deeply loving—another child. In the midst of the plague, she attempts to build a home, maintain Goldmund as her husband; she carries within her his child. But there are times for life and times for death: a gray-haired, lank, powerful stranger mauls her breasts. The next day, she begins to die from the plague, visibly turning from child to grandmother. Yet her stature is greater than Robert's; she assumes the expression of the death-mother, her face contorted in horror and delight as Goldmund joyfully slaughters the rapist. That night he sees her face in the moon, a mother-face with "wide, large eyes full of lust and murder" (p. 214). Even the woman as life-bearer can paiticipate in death fully and naturally; Robert runs from death.

Goldmund is the only one of the trio to survive. He

accepts death, understands it, sees both its beauty and horror, its meaning, and as an artist he transcends it. Goldmund's first encounter with the plague—his entry into the farm of death—is one of the most remarkable passages in the book. The corpses of the old woman, the farmer and his wife, their son and daughter are like his statues: depending on the individual, they preserve in themselves horror, fury, suffering, stubborn control, or fear. Each is beautiful to him; each corpse preserves its life's last, individual, touching and heroic expression. But corpses decay. Only the artist can preserve. Goldmund stores the images. This desire to preserve preserves *him* through the plague. By its conclusion, he has virtually lost the will to live. His only motivation for continuing existence is curiosity, the artist's hunger for experience, the artist's drive to embody that experience in an eternal form that speaks to the spirit of man.

These revelations do not come all at once. Goldmund begins as a wanderer, a man suited to survive death, for he can live in the transitory. He sees the beauty of death in the farmhouse. Wandering through the country, he lives in abundance upon the possessions of the dead. Wandering through the city, he finds a wife and per- suades her to build with him. Ready to leave her and return to the artist's life and then to Narcissus (as he eventually will), he loses her and enters into the greatest horror of all: the country-wide insanity of fear-driven men. He sees families desert one another; he sees rape, looting, reversion to the primitive, the isolation of each fear-driven person, the madness of the death dance, and —most horrible of all—the torture and slaughter of scape- goats, the pillaging of the ghettos, and the killing of the Jews. Throwing himself into the death dance, eating and making love among the dying, Goldmund has exhausted all desire to live, and is ready to return to Meister Nik- laus. Then he meets Rebekka, the beautiful Jewish girl whose father has been murdered in a pogrom. He urges her to live with him and love him, but she angrily rejects him. She is the sister of Lydia: one in love with love, the other in love with death. Both are virgins. Both live in the houses of their fathers. Both of their lives lead away from the vitality that is the other half of Goldmund's being. Both lead him to the realization of the beauty of the complete yet unexperienced woman: the virgin of life yet unrealized, the virgin of death never realized. Despite their femininity, the proud Jewish girl and the knight's daughter come closer to the spiritual life of the father than any other woman Goldmund encounters: "To love such women brought suffering. But for a while it seemed to him as though he had never loved any other women" (p. 224).

After his encounter with Rebekka, Goldmund passes a church and sees its stone figures. He had always thought the wood of Niklaus preferable to stone because of the vitality of the mother-material. But now he sees in the frozen stone, symbol of the eternal Self, a greater permanence and power than wood could ever attain. He enters the church to confess his sins, but his confession turns into an attack upon God for the chaos of the earth. Outside, he looks up at the stone figures once more and vows to bring through his art a meaning to that chaos. It was man, not God, who created these figures: "immobile, inaccessible, superhuman . . . an infinite consolation, a triumphant victory over death and despair as they stood in their dignity and beauty, surviving one dying generation of men after another" (p. 227).

But Goldmund is not yet prepared for the moment of artistic maturity and harvest; he must complete his life by living its ranges at their fullest intensity. His love and loss of Agnes completes human experience for him. Before I treat the Agnes episode, however, I want to sum up Goldmund's present state as an artist. The bare facts are that he doesn't have a workshop because of Meister Niklaus' death. But through the circumstances of that death and through Marie, Hesse suggests deeper implications.

When he returns to the bishop's city, Goldmund is ready for art, a state which the city reflects: its citizens are happy and secure again, the sun is out, golden fish glimmer in the murky river. But then, after the Niklaus episode, the sun has set, the water is cold, and the fish are gone; Goldmund is again aware of death. The circumstances of Niklaus' death are significant; he died not from plague but from the effort of caring for his afflicted daughter, who emerged from her illness a "shy, bent-over old maid" (p. 231). I think that Lisbeth represents the quality of the Meister's artistic nature: it is hoarded and exploited for material purposes satisfactory to the city-dweller. The Meister has taken a course which will finally stifle his creativity, insofar as it belongs to the world of the mother. It is through the mother-world—the plague—that he is afflicted first; her route to him is to destroy the father-exploited feminine qualities of creativity. His talent gone, he cannot survive; he dies and he leaves behind him something once proud and beautiful but now clearly weak and infertile, as it always was.

As Lisbeth was to the Meister, so Marie seems to be to Goldmund. She is connected with the artistic impulse in that she provides him the materials to work upon; in her house hangs a madonna that he once painted, as a city-artist. Her qualities are more positive than Lisbeth's; she is loving, gentle, provides for him, gives him some security and assurance, arranges for the release of the artistic urge through her materials, allows him to fix the images of his life permanently. She has the beautiful dark eyes that Goldmund saw in the childlike virgin he first loved. But Marie, though maturer and more beautiful, is as she was before the plague: she is lame. Goldmund is fond of her, and she yearns for health and strength so that he will not follow other women, but he cannot love her. He leaves her easily for Agnes. The character of Marie has three implications: insofar as Goldmund has learned his art from the Meister, it is insufficient for his purposes; art practiced in the city for the city is imperfect (Marie lives near the fish-market where Goldmund has often pondered the exploitation of fecundity); and Goldmund's experience is not yet fully formed.

The Agnes episode epitomizes the double-theme of life and death for Goldmund. Correspondingly, his experience with her has two phases, one before and one after Halloween: the life-phase is the ecstasy of his union with her the first evening; the death-phase is the horror of extinction that he experiences on the second evening, which ends in the dungeon. The context of both is the world of the father, represented successively by Count Heinrich and the priests. Count Heinrich's presence has changed the city from the holy city that it was when the bishop had resided there; he is a proud "courtier and warrior" (p. 231), right hand of the Emperor, disliked by the oppressed people, the symbol of masculine power and organization, a man significantly like Goldmund's own father. Goldmund will become impotent against him; only Narcissus will be able to redeem Goldmund from the paralysis, fear, and impending death with which Heinrich punishes him.

While Heinrich resembles Goldmund's father, Agnes is quite explicitly like his mother. At first sight of her, he doesn't realize this fact; he is stunned by the charismatic impact of her pride, strength, and sensuality. At the close of this first encounter, he realizes that she is not only his equal in sensuality and spirit, wildness and delicacy, but except that she is female, she is exactly like him; she has his features, his blond hair, his blue eyes. He immediately shaves and cuts his hair to enhance the resemblance. Initially, Agnes appears as an ideal anima projection—the woman every man loves. But Goldmund's wisdom takes him deeper; he realizes that she is not outside him, she is within him. Goldmund has recognized the anima within himself, cultivated it, virtually become hermaphroditic as he has followed the course of his mother through all of her various stages. He is nearing completion.

On the day that they decide to become lovers, Goldmund progresses a step further. Agnes' "tall figure and blond joyful energy reminded him of the image of his mother as he once, as a boy in Mariabronn, carried it

131

in his heart" (p. 240). He has offered himself to her and has assured her that he will face death to share a single moment of ecstasy with her. As a pass into her castle, she has given him a chain, a complex symbol signifying human matrimony, the marriage of heaven and earth, the integration of society and psyche. But, as he leaves, there is an ominous image: golden leaves are falling from the autumnal trees. Goldmund thinks of them only as the end of his despair, but the falling of the golden leaf also predicts the loss of happiness (the leaf) and of a vauable spiritual state obtained during the plague (the gold).

The night that they first make love is dense with symbolism emphasizing the significance of this merging with the mother through the anima. Outside the room, the priests talk interminably with the lord. Blues appear in Agnes' dress, the lovers' eyes, the wine glass. Whites appear in fur and wine. The lovers eat together and drink from the same glass. Goldmund is to Agnes a bird and a musician. The image-pattern suggests that this union is of as deep spiritual significance as the concerns of the priestly spirits outside. Whites and blues, a frequent symbolic contrast, carry many undertones. Perhaps dominant among these, blue signifies the mystic center, and white suggests the moon color with all the moon's relationships to the mother: the instinctive, the irrational, the mystic, the intuitive, and death. The eucharistic meal is accompanied by the lunar white wine. Agnes' naming Goldmund her bird and her musician implies that she regards him as a principle of the artistic soul and imagination that will complete her mother-world and elevate it to the realm of the spiritual. But the musician is not only symbolic of the intermediate realm between earth and heaven; he is also commonly a figure of death enchanting his followers like the Pied Piper into that state at its most attractive. Whether or not this last implication is present in Agnes' love-term, it is certainly dominant in her mind at the peak of their ecstasy:

"I want to have a child by you, sweet Goldmund.
And still more, I'd like to die with you. Drink
me to the dregs, beloved, melt me, kill me!"
(p. 242).

But Goldmund rejects her:

"I don't feel like dying, I don't want to be killed
by your count. First I want us to be as happy as
we have been today. One more time, many more
times" (p. 242).

Although there are many undertones to Goldmund's
rejection—fear of the father, an inadequate reconciliation
with death—Hesse gives the explicit reason during Goldmund's hike into the mountains the next day. There, in
the realm of the spiritual, Goldmund reviews his whole
life: both its sensual and murderous phase (Lene, Robert,
Viktor) and its spiritual phase (the cloister, the castle,
Rebekka). His painful conclusion is that all is transitory.
He feels a great need to create something from his life,
beyond Narcissus as Saint John. Progressing from the
conflict between the life of nature and the life of the
artist, Goldmund sees a great opposition within human
experience: man/woman, gypsy/citizen, intellectual/sen-
sualist. This split most keenly afflicts the male; whereas
a woman can realize herself by bearing a child out of
her sensuality, a man must choose between sensuality
and creativity, life and art. The longing to synthesize the
split dominates Goldmund. And even this longing itself is
dual: it causes great anguish and discontent even as it
produces "all that was beautiful and holy, all that man
created and gave back to God as a sacrifice of thanks"
(p. 247). Agnes could die in a moment of mystic perception of the union of love, birth, and death. But Goldmund
must live past that moment for his fulfillment: the defeat
of the transitory and the synthesis of the universe through
the artistic act.
But Goldmund dismisses these somber thoughts: "As

long as his life was a garden in which such magic flowers as Agnes bloomed, he had no reason to complain" (p. 248). He has not yet fully realized the implications of his relationship with the mother. As Agnes implied, the mystic ecstasy will bring death as well as life. When he meets her again, she has changed into an anxious and fearful woman who reminds him of Lydia, the virgin who led him to murder Viktor. Events rapidly develop this hint into a reality; he is caught by Count Heinrich. But though he rejected the mother's invitation the night before, he does not betray her to the father tonight, for although his artist's nature differs from hers, it requires hers for its sustenance. He would rather die as a thief. And it is the mother who has led him to his death.

However, it is the father who will execute it—as a grim and horrible necessity. His symbols surround and frighten and blind Goldmund: swords, candles, flame. He will hang the thief, the hanged man being not ony the sacrificial victim but another symbol of Goldmund as intermediary between mother and father—the dead man suspended between earth and heaven. Goldmund's paralysis and entry into the horrifying areas of the unconscious are conveyed by the binding ropes and the frightening dungeon. He begs for light but is refused, for light passes as quickly as life and will be of no use to a dying man.

In the dungeon, Goldmund first tries to reconcile himself to death, then sleeps, and wakes with thoughts of murder as he determines to live. In the moments before sleep, his mind is full of the beautiful images of the mother: his woman, his art, his body, hills, sun, sky, stars, forests, seasons, birds, fish, dancing boys, farms, wine, walnuts. He cannot leave this beautiful world of the living and he breaks into tears like "a disconsolate boy." He prays: "Oh mother, oh mother!" (p. 254). A vision of his real mother appears, as beautiful and as gentle as she once was. He submits. He gives all that he has loved to her. Then he sleeps. But when he wakes, his mood has changed. He is most acutely aware of the paralysis and pain in his arms. He becomes violently committed to life, but, ironically, his thoughts are of murder as they were when he struggled to live under Viktor's assault. Until the very end of his days, death will give rise to life; life will give rise to death. But his hostility is directed towards men—the guards who will kill him, the priest he will murder to get free—and towards God himself. He begins to manage the deepest horror of the unconscious; he frees himself from the ropes and acquaints himself with the dungeon. He is now in tune with his environment; his will is strong enough to take the last murderous chance to survive. But the priest who comes in with two candles—one for each of them—is Narcissus.

There only remains one more adventure in the mother-world for Goldmund, and it will kill him—with his consent this time. The rest of the novel shows Goldmund in the father-world, introducing its intellectual spirit to his artistic spirit, synthesizing it with the mother-world. Goldmund's spring and summer are over. There will be no more Lise and Lydia and Viktor, no more city-loves and city-brawling, no more Lene and the plague, no more Agnes. Her two days of violent ecstasy and violent horror have brought the dualities of his life into powerful opposition. The only keener experience that world could have offered him would have been the death in orgasm which Agnes yearned for. He rejected this because of his longing to transcend the oppositions and transitoriness of her world. He must return to the world of the father to accomplish this. But Goldmund will never desert the world of the mother. He needs the mother for the autumnal harvest of his experience.

There is actually a double autumnal harvest: Goldmund's harvest of art from his experience and Narcissus' harvest of love from seeds he planted in Goldmund. But one is sweet and the other bitter; Goldmund will enter his winter a completed man, but Narcissus must remain incomplete.

Goldmund's recovery begins when he recognizes Narcissus. His voice and bearing molding themselves to

135

those of his rescuer, Goldmund becomes proud, controlled, and ironic before a man who has the great stature stemming from his self-realization as spiritual leader of his cloister. Narcissus is also a political power who can bargain successfully with Count Heinrich for Goldmund's freedom. Once back at the cloister, Goldmund receives further spiritual insight; he not only regains his old love for the community of the fathers, but he sees in the art of the cloister a unity of spirit beyond the father or the mother. He feels that he will never surpass the beauty of this integrated world of stone. Yet, with Narcissus' encouragement, he prepares to make his contribution. He will carve a staircase panel embodying the dual world of spirit and of nature which he has experienced. Nature is intricate, varied, beautiful, complex. Spirit is represented best by the carving of Father Daniel as one of the evangelists.

Conversations between Goldmund and Narcissus open the way further for each man to understand himself. Though Goldmund begins by reacting to the evil in the world, he sees that he is simply feeling the bad moment that he is in and that he will cycle back to a perception of the good that will come. He sees most clearly now that his art is not only a defense against the transitory that has so afflicted him but an insight into the basic nature and problem of humanity. Narcissus teaches him that in this way the artist and the thinker unite; they differ only in that the one uses the sensual image and the other the abstraction. Although neither mode is perfect, both lead to self-realization as they are used to comprehend the ultimate being—whether in the form of Siddhartha's Atman, Narcissus' God, or Goldmund's Mother. Narcissus further educates Goldmund by teaching him the mode of contemplation—a Christian version of Siddhartha's meditation; Goldmund learns to free himself from the exhausting isolation of the active artist and enter into a renovating state of childlike innocence, into a perception of the calmness of the universe beyond artist's image or thinker's abstraction.

Meanwhile, through these conversations, through his growing *feeling* of the importance of art, through his growing pleasure in Goldmund, Narcissus is beginning to develop. Goldmund teaches him the same lesson that he had long ago taught to the artist: the necessity of love. Narcissus comes to love the mother as she appears in Goldmund, comes to respect the powers she gives him, comes to admire the courage, nobility, difficulty, and humanity in the artist's life. Finally, he even begins to doubt that his mode of perception is equal to Goldmund's, for art is more innocent and childlike, more loving of God in embracing His world rather than analyzing it, and more sacrificial of self upon the cross of human experience.

Rehabilitated, Goldmund expends his experience in the intricate carvings of the panel and then in a carving of Lydia as the Virgin Mary. Through these acts of creation he not only embodies the universal in his experience but communicates it. Narcissus first feels the deepest understanding of Goldmund and art when he sees the carving of the saintly Abbot Daniel; and through the example of his life, Goldmund gains and educates a student, Erich, who will carry on his impulse and his craft. But, as Goldmund had learned in the bishop's city, the artistic act sustains the artist's life only as long as he creates. When it is done, he is totally emptied of experience. He must either gain more or, like Niklaus, die both as man and artist. So Goldmund, aging and exhausted, returns to the mother-world to restore himself with its experience.

Goldmund's absence brings Narcissus' development to its completion. First, he feels affectionate pride and gratitude because of the protegé who has become his equal, and in his imagination he vicariously enjoys the rascal's exploits. But as Goldmund's absence continues, Narcissus begins to feel longing, worry and guilt that he has not yet told Goldmund of his love for him. Ultimately, he begins to feel weaker and more doubtful about his way of existence as he begins to understand that a man can enter the deepest sin—as he had never dared to do—and not extinguish the divine within himself. Although Narcissus realizes that he must continue following the course that Self dictates, he has lost the pride in self that Abbot Daniel had always thought his greatest weakness. Goldmund has broken into his isolation.

Goldmund finally returns, an aged man prepared to die. In one of the most compelling scenes of the novel,

> Narcissus, his heart burning with grief and love, slowly bent down to him, and now he did what he had never done in the many years of their friendship. He touched Goldmund's hair and forehead with his lips (p. 306).

He confesses,

> "I have been able to love you, you alone among all men. You cannot imagine what that means. It means a well in a desert, a blossoming tree in the wilderness . . . a place within me has remained open to grace" (p. 306).

Goldmund is in need of this love. He has visited Agnes, been rejected by her, fallen from his horse and crushed his chest, and suffered a terrible pain that has made him into an old man. But Goldmund is prepared for death. And he has learned the lesson from the mother. In a sense, he becomes like other old men in Hesse's work—a Vasudeva, an Abbot Daniel. He impresses Narcissus with his contentment, his detachment, and his surrender. And he has the kindly humor of the wise man. His death will not be tragic. It will be the completion of a full life.

Goldmund explains to Narcissus that the Mother has taught him what each man must learn—how to die. She has filled his life and ended his desire by being all women and all experience to him:

". . . my mother called me and I had to follow.
She is everywhere. She was Lise, the gypsy; she
was Master Niklaus' beautiful madonna; she
was life, love, ecstasy. She also was fear, hunger, instinct. Now she is death; she has her fin-
gers in my chest" (p. 310).

Still, she is multiple: she works to take his heart from
him in moods of ecstasy or laughter, or gentleness. It is
her sadness, the sadness of the moon among clouds, that
draws him most to death. He now knows her completely,
for he has accepted her death aspect as he never could
as a young man. Nor has he only left life—he also has
left art. He cannot and will not carve the completed
mother. To know her is to die. To "make her secret visible" through his art would be to end that secret, the mystery of which beautifies and empowers all life and art
from the glinting fish in the murky city river to the
enigmatic smile of pain and joy on the face of Niklaus'
madonna. Finally, he faces death as a completion, and
he yearns for it in the hope that it "will be a great
happiness, a happiness as great as that of love, fulfilled
love" (p. 308). Both are the same. Both unify in the
mother as she draws Goldmund back to the state that was
the beginning and will be the end of all: "nonbeing and
innocence" (p. 308).

A completed man, Goldmund dies, his question burn-
ing "like fire" in Narcissus' heart:

But how will you die when your time comes,
Narcissus, since you have no mother? (p. 311).

As Goldmund learned in the count's dungeon, death needs
as much preparation as does any other of the major
human acts: birth, love, art, thought. As the mother-world
of life, love, ecstasy, horror, hunger, and instinct nurtured
and trained the vitality in Goldmund's body and spirit,
so it has eased and then exhausted them so that he dies
within nature as gently as did Abbot Daniel. Through

art, he has risen as high in the realm of the spirit as has Narcissus. Through his death, he has surpassed him. Narcissus will have to "die" too: he must now begin the journey through the thousand selves.

CHAPTER FOUR

Magister Ludi: The Schoolmaster

In *Magister Ludi,* Hesse shows how Narcissus will die. Set in the future, this novel presents the career of Joseph Knecht, the finest representative of human knowledge, as he works out his fate in the twilight of the Age of Reason.[1] At the outset, the period seems far from a "twilight": through synthesis of all intellectual disciplines and development of an elite intelligentsia, the intellectual has freed himself from all bondage to society except an economic one which at the moment exacts no repressive control over the intellectual establishment centered at

Castalia; the damage caused by twentieth-century political and military control of the intellectual has brought society to its senses. The intellectual is free. But he uses his freedom to worship Truth in itself in the form of the Glass Bead Game ruled by its priest, Castalia's most influential member, the Master of the Game—the Magister Ludi. Truth worshipped without an ethical obligation to human nature becomes, however, worship of something else: Beauty, a beauty of the symmetry and harmony of the systems of Truth appealing alike to the pure mathematician and the pure musician. Meanwhile, society is left to its own devices. Human nature responds to itself alone. And war rumbles.

Joseph Knecht, whose name means "servant," will sacrifice himself to demonstrate to Castalia its danger. He is a man so completely devoted to his vocation that he has become the human embodiment of the Game. What it is and can be and will not be determines his life and death; he has the beauty of the Game and its awareness of the relationship of Truth to the Whole, he has its inclination to descend from Truth-as-Beauty to include Nature in its sphere to realize it as an embodiment of the Whole, and he has its terrible vulnerability. His effort to include Nature is a failure. He dies. The Game will vanish. But through Knecht's sacrifice, humanity's awareness of the beauty, truth, and reality of the Whole will continue to remain the goal of human evolution.

In the following pages, after discussing the plot of *Magister Ludi* and before I concentrate on Joseph Knecht, I will focus on two particularly difficult problems in the novel: the natures of the Game itself and of music. When I turn to Knecht, I will show that Knecht, as human embodiment of the Game, sacrifices himself to teach by example the lesson of the "Schoolmaster," the archetypal Teacher such as Buddha and Christ. While it is necessary that the great cultures must die because they cannot embody the Whole, it is equally necessary that human society must continue until it transcends its own nature and becomes one with the cosmos. Harry Haller's doctrine of the thousand souls becomes generalized in *Magister Ludi* to a theory of human history. In his fourth "life," Hesse transcends the concerns of such elect individuals as the mystic Siddhartha, the schizophrenic Harry, and the artist Goldmund, in order to address himself to the whole species.

Magister Ludi is a biography of Joseph Knecht written around 2400 A.D. by an anonymous monk.[2] Both the biographer and Knecht are members of Castalia, one of several German states containing systems of secular schools. Castalia is the capital of the system; it trains the country's elite students, the best of whom form an administration controlling the whole educational system. Joseph Knecht's career illustrates the operations of the system. At twelve, Knecht is a student in an ordinary school in a small town. Since he shows a remarkable aptitude for music, his teacher recommends his admittance into a Castalian elite school; the Music Master himself, the man in control of Germany's entire musical culture, interviews Knecht and recommends him for entry into Eschholz where he survives rugged competition to become, at seventeen, one of the few assigned to a Castalian university, Waldzell. Waldzell educates the "elite of the elite" (p. 74), no more than sixty students from the whole country.

Waldzell emphasizes the arts and their relationship to other disciplines, and it is the seat of the Glass Bead Game; it trains the Game's players, houses its administration, and is the location of its ritual performances. The Glass Bead Game is a ceremony partially academic and partially religious in character. Although Knecht's biographer states that its details are too complex for the layman to comprehend, its basis seems to be a symbolic language uniting the content and methods of all the arts and sciences; as the twentieth century logic so important to our computers has derived from a merging of logic and mathematics, so did the Game derive from a merging of mathematical and musical symbolic systems, which in turn was extended to express and unify the rest of the academic disciplines.[3] Its potential is limitless; it can produce "the entire intellectual content of the universe" through infinite combinations of themes from different disciplines brought into different harmonies unique to the individual player (p. 7). The Game is taught and played daily in Waldzell classes, and each spring the "Magister Ludi," a chief Castalian administrator, conducts a special Game before the assembled intelligentsia and broadcast to the whole world.

Rather than immediately studying the Game, Knecht begins to master the art of meditation and continues to specialize in music for two or three years, to the distress of the headmaster, who urges him to take a more general course of studies. During this period Knecht also undergoes the traumatic experience of having to defend the Castalian establishment against the attacks of a future politician, Plinio Designori. Whereas the successful graduates of Waldzell will spend the rest of their lives in Castalia as intellectual "monks" without families, worldly occupations, or even permission to visit the outside world, Designori is an "outsider," a visitor to Waldzell who will return to a normal university. The debates fortify doubts that Knecht has had about his vocation, doubts he expresses in a slim volume of poems appended to the biography.

After graduation from Waldzell, Knecht like others is given an indeterminate period of free study while he decides if he wishes to enter into the Castalian order. Unlike the others, however, Knecht withdraws from sight until he is thirty-five, during which time he tests the premises and operations of the Glass Bead Game thoroughly and spends a period learning Chinese and the methods and import of the *I Ching* from Elder Brother, an eccentric who lives in a self-designed hermitage. Performing one of the few required Castalian assignments, Knecht also writes three *Lives* in which he projects his personality into different historical periods. Appended

144

also to the biography, these *Lives* depict Knecht in the roles of a neolithic rainmaker serving a matriarchal community which eventually sacrifices him, an early medieval desert monk who learns self-abnegation from an older monk, and a young Indian nobleman who learns from a yogi that the world is illusory. Through these lives run the themes of self-realization, harmony with the cosmos, service of a society which martyrs or neglects the intellectual, and the necessity of the teacher who passes on universal truths.

During his life, Knecht has continually displayed a charisma that has attracted others to him, a power which has disturbed him greatly and delayed his commitment to the Game. The charismatic quality eventually attracts the aristocratic Magister Ludi, Thomas von der Trave, who tests Knecht and invites him into the Order. Knecht accepts and soon after is given his first assignment: to introduce the Game to the monks of a Benedictine monastery at Mariafels. It develops, however, that the real reason for the post is an effort by the usually apolitical Castalia to intitiate a relationship with the other great educational and spiritual force in Germany, the Catholic Church. Without forethought, Knecht impresses the leading political power in Mariafels, the ancient Father Jacobus, who in turn introduces Knecht to history and to the possibility that Castalia has deserted its ethical responsibility to society through an aristocratic commitment to knowledge for knowledge's sake.

After completing his task at Mariafels and winning an annual Glass Bead Game contest, Knecht applies for and receives permission to resume life at Castalia. When he returns, the Magister Ludi suddenly dies and, at the early age of forty, Knecht wins the post. He performs magnificently, winning vital acceptance from the elite students, mastering his administrative duties, employing his charisma to unite the members of his hierarchy, and devising with his iconoclastic friend Tegularius one of the finest and most beautiful of all Games, the Chinese House Game. During this period, he is witness to the death of

145

his old friend the Music Master, whose life of service and meditation has brought him to the sanctity of Self-realization (in both Jungian and Siddharthian terms); through embodying music, the Master realizes the Whole.

Knecht's continuing doubts mount about Castalia's social relevance, its methods and goals of education, its use of the Glass Bead Game, its very possibility of survival. These come to a head when he once again meets Plinio Designori and sees how badly the politician's education in Waldzell has fitted him for his personal and public life. These failures combine with Knecht's own sense that in order to attain Self-realization he must enter the society he has never known and serve that society as a teacher of ordinary people. He shocks Castalia with a circular letter in which he submits his resignation with a warning to the educational system to change its course or be destroyed by society.

Knecht's first job in the outside world is to educate Plinio's unruly son, Tito. Having already obtained rapport with the boy while he was disengaging from Castalia, Knecht spends his first day with him in a cabin by a lake in the mountains. Tito challenges his weary teacher to swim the icy lake with him. Committed to winning his student's respect, Knecht accepts the challenge. Within a few minutes, fighting vigorously until the last, Knecht drowns.

This plot can be divided into two periods: Knecht's passive student years and his more active years as a Castalian monk and Magister Ludi. If the "Posthumous Writings" are included in the student years and "The Legend" is included in the years as Magister Ludi, it develops that there is about equal stress on each period. I will make the same stress. Since the biographer's style is rather dry, a reader may find the novel more rewarding if he reads the "Posthumous Writings" twice: first at the points in Knecht's student career when they were written; Knecht is a much more complex and interesting character than the biographer understands him to be.

146

The second time, they should be read as a continuation of "The Legend"; their mysteries and those of the Legend will clarify one another. I will write here as I recommend reading *Magister Ludi;* I will treat "The Posthumous Writings" twice—the results are quite surprising.

The biographer threatens to do more than bore us. He can mislead us rather badly about Knecht. He gives us the "public view": notes from Knecht's lectures, letters by him and about him, reports in official records. The problem of finding Knecht in this material is further complicated by the fact that the biographer is an "establishment" Castalian beyond whose vision Knecht eventually moves; for the post-Castalian events he can only print a student "legend." But attention to Knecht's biographer can produce many amusing moments if one observes the distance between him and his subject—even greater than that between X and Harry Haller.

We can't simply write off Knecht's biographer as a fool. Knecht has had an impact on him. Castalia had virtually no knowledge of its historical roots and its human quality in the pre-Knecht period; its emphasis upon the universal forbade attention to the mother-world of the private, the subjective, the accidental and transitory. That the biographer is writing at all is a definite response to Knecht's call for historical awareness; biographies are unusual in Castalia. And the narrator is not only deeply concerned about the meaning of Knecht's existence to Castalia; he is also strongly attracted to the man and his values, despite his historian's commitment to objectivity. He is perceptive enough to see the value of the subjective Legend, poems, and Lives, but still Castalian enough to look upon the poems with considerable disapproval.

A further complication is the biographer's own development from the elitist of the introduction to one who can sympathetically present Plinio Designori's case—although right until the end of his biography he maintains an ironic attitude toward the anti-establishment Tegularius. In short, the biographer is not only a developing character, but during his development he is often ambiv-

147

alent. I will try to extract the "truth" of Knecht from the biographer's presentation. But before I turn to that task, I want to explain some particularly difficult areas in the novel: the subjects of the Glass Bead Game and music. Since these are the vocations which Knecht and the Music Master, respectively, will come to personify, it is necessary to have a clear grasp of their natures and their significance.

The Glass Bead Game came into being because human history was prepared for it. Four hundred years before the events of the novel, twentieth-century society (the Age of the Feuilleton) collapsed because "it did not know how to assign culture its proper place within the economy of life and the nation" (p. 9). Our ancestors had fought bloody wars to free human reason from the bondage of the church. But with the authority of this institution and the similarly restrictive state undermined, men could not create an institution which would re-order society by embodying the intellectual freedom they had obtained, for their conception of freedom did not include a commitment to intellectual responsibility. Accordingly, those who didn't seek intellectual freedom were deprived of two institutions in return for none:

> they faced death, fear, pain, and hunger almost without defenses, could no longer accept the consolations of the churches, and could obtain no useful advice from Reason (p. 13).

Human life became in the twentieth century a retreat into an imaginary world; its culture provided crossword puzzles and superficial articles and lectures (the Feuilleton); it was dead, and the society itself would soon die. Its music—clearest expression of the cultural soul—became demonic, chaotic, fragmented, dissonant, obscure. Its people became cynical, anti-intellectual, pessimistic; they threw themselves into the dance of death or quietly retreated in despair. The economy crumbled; the politicians and generals ruled; social chaos and war erupted to clear away the rubbish of the dead society. During this period of destruction, the intellectual further betrayed the Mind; he sold himself to the highest bidder, to the politician or general who demanded that he serve state or war-effort. Although it may have seemed to the intellectual that he was serving society, in serving material interests he had to compromise intellectual honesty by subordinating theory to practice, truth to practicality. Accordingly, the intellectual did the last, greatest injury to his society: having deprived it of Faith, he now deprived it of Truth. In the period of recovery, the state and the people returned education to the new intelligentsia that had developed, for the whole economic, technological and professional system had become dangerously inefficient for lack of the "pure and keen" thinking that only those committed to preservation of truth can provide.

The new intelligentsia began among the scholars of musical science and mathematics and in the mystic League of Journeyers to the East.[4] The one fostered an intellectual discipline, the other a spiritual discipline through "mystic identification with remote ages and cultural conditions" that kept alive humanity's perception of the Whole. Among these early musical scientists developed the Glass Bead Game, a system of representing a wide variety of musical elements and their relationships through differently shaped and colored beads strung on a frame which looked like an abacus; later, the mathematicians and astronomers took over the Game and used it to express the processes of their disciplines by its symbols. They were followed by linguists, logicians, physicists; then entered the theoreticians of the arts, architecture and the "visual arts" (p. 23).

The Game became a focus for the intelligentsia's most stringent application of the skills of its discipline. It also became a keen intellectual pleasure compensating for the elite intellectual's rejection of the world; he had become in effect a "monk" belonging to an Order, rather than

149

a discipline, and conducted an aloof and austere life solely devoted to the pursuit of truth.

Finally, one man, Lusor Basiliensis, constructed a single symbolic language expressing the content of all disciplines that had been able to use the Glass Bead Game; and he managed to do so in a way that allowed each individual person to express his individuality and imagination in manipulating the processes and contents of these disciplines. The last important development came from the mystic League; it contributed the techniques and the goal of meditation. The Glass Bead Game now gained a "religious spirit" as it affirmed not only the relationship of each discipline to the other but to the Whole. Soon the Game became a public ceremonial conducted by the Magister Ludi, who was its high priest. Intellectuals from all disciplines would live a highly-ritualized life during the period of the Game; during its performance they would meditate on each symbol as the Magister Ludi's drawing of each would be projected on a large screen before them; a "low, throbbing base bell-note" established a mesmeric rhythmical background.

By this time, the intelligentsia's monastic order had complete control of the country's intellectual and cultural life, for the state had realized their importance. Through "pedagogical provinces" the Orders staffed and administered secular schools at all levels, controlled the intellectual life of the country in other areas, and devoted themselves to the preservation and continuation of the culture so disastrously threatened in the twentieth century; the Glass Bead Game was the highest expression of their commitment to the intellect. The province providing the central administrators of the educational system—Castalia—contained Waldzell, which housed the Game and trained players recruited from the elite of the elite. The Magister Ludi became a central power in the administration, matched only by the President, who was an accomplished meditator deriving from the old League influence.

The Game is difficult to describe, for it is a closed

system of symbols which have no single and abiding relationship to the concrete phenomena of our lives. And unlike other such closed systems (e.g., music and mathematics), we don't even know what the symbols are —Hesse never tells us beyond stressing the beauty of the calligraphy in Knecht's Chinese House Game. Consisting of both symbols and a "grammar" of their relationships, it is an immensely difficult discipline to learn, for it requires wide acquaintance with the basics of all the member disciplines. Its grammar, however, has the simplicity, consistency, and symmetry of a scientific grammar such as modern linguistic transformationalists are attempting to construct, or—to give an example probably much closer to the game—the symbolic language of our modern computers.

And the number of symbols and the operations of the system are strictly controlled by a Games Commission, a restriction that no more diminishes its infinite possibilities than does limiting our alphabet to twenty-six letters. The individual is so much in control of a specific Game that it is rare that two games, even with the same basic input, will ever be alike; the Game is capable of expressing "the entire intellectual content" of the universe (p. 7). Although Games used to exploit highly complex possibilities, now they are basically simple: they will begin with one to three themes from one of the member disciplines (e.g., music and biology), interweave them, and ultimately relate them. Particularly popular in the past—and presently with Knecht—is the harmonizing of opposites, such as freedom and law.

Although many Castalians incline strongly toward creating abstract but beautiful patterns, the Games still consistently end in establishing harmony and unity, testifying to Wholeness in the universe. That they rigidly avoid jarring, chaotic, and pessimistic material is not due to the limitations of the Game any more than it is to those of music; it is an expression of the affirmative nature of this society. Typically a Game moves from becoming to being; it establishes the potentiality of its symbols first, next the necessary conditions which they must conform to, then the possible relationships between them that further determine this necessity, and finally a conclusion in which the necessary potentialities of combination are realized.

This unity is typically realized by one of two different kinds of Games: the formal or the psychological. Although he constructs one to prove to himself that he can do it, Knecht doesn't prefer the formal Game; it simply tries to represent universal perfection and unity by representing it in a "form"—a beautifully perfect and unified system. Knecht values more the psychological Game—which is what his famous Chinese House Game apparently is—because it stresses meditation upon an organized series of symbols that eventually leads to a *vision* of the perfection and unity of the Whole. In other words, Knecht desires that the Game have relevance to the players.

The infrequency of such relevance, particularly social relevance, is Knecht's special concern. The Game already has some serious disadvantages. Although it demands a basic grasp of a discipline's content and methods (e.g., musical theory), it doesn't require that the player master a discipline—become a musician. Accordingly, to follow the example, it does not take account of the sensuousness of music—the sounds and their physical, emotional, and psychological impact. The Game requires that a player grasp the spirit of music but not necessarily its substance. One of the dangers here is that during historical periods of degeneration, substance dominates the spirit: the Game's emphasis upon harmony and unity makes Castalians singularly vulnerable to the possibility of chaos—and such a possibility is presently simmering in twenty-fourth century society, very likely because of Castalia's aloofness. In short, through love of the Game Castalia rejects Goldmund's mother-world—even the necessity of coping with it—and focuses entirely on the father-world of Narcissus.

But the austere Castalians don't display the ethical awareness of a Narcissus; his act of service to Goldmund is not so important to them. If a Castalian isn't an aesthete concerned with the formal beauty of the Game, he is generally a mystic lost in contemplation of the universal mysteries that the Game approaches. Such a mystical vision is absolutely necessary, but it is highly dubious, in the opinions of both the Music Master and Knecht, that it can be reached through withdrawal; it involves *acting* in the world, realizing the Self through such action (living the thousand lives). Acting for both men means *teaching*. The difference between these two men and the average Castalian is the difference between a man who affirms the reality of his religion by living it and men who do so by mystic withdrawal or, more dangerous, rapt absorption in the beauty of church ritual and ceremonies. Withdrawal and beauty will come only *after* action is no longer possible.

That the Castalians believe otherwise not only diminishes the profound significance of the Game as a symbol of universal perfection and unity by its exclusion of "life" but it also endangers the very being of the Game should that unattended life which supports it cease to do so. Knecht expresses it simply in his circular letter: the state will take the money away for the wars that the Game didn't avert.

Despite both intuitions and, finally, clear knowledge about the dangers of the Game, Knecht will commit himself to it to such an extent that when he leaves it, he will die. He chooses to serve the Game because it is his "calling" (the translation of *vocation*), the calling of the Self that demands to be realized; by heredity and environment, he is perfectly suited for it. But the Game is not suited for survival. The peaceful death of the ancient Music Master suggests that music is. To better understand the failures of the Game, we should consider the very similar but significantly different calling of the Music Master.

Music is a better representation of the universal Whole. On the one hand, its abstract nature, closed system, non-referential character, and logic make it an apt symbol of the Spirit, the world of the father. On the other hand, its sensuous quality, its actual sounds entering the human senses and matching themselves to the rhythms of the human lungs and heart, and its impact upon the emotions make it an equally apt symbol of Nature, the world of the mother. But, most important, music can transcend this dualism and become a symbol of the Whole:

> Music arises from Measure and is rooted in the great Oneness. The Great Oneness begets the two poles; the two poles beget the power of Darkness and of Light (p. 19).

Music's responsiveness to the great universal dualities make it most receptive (though not vulnerable) to the nature of any given society. When a society is disintegrating, its music becomes fragmented, discordant, deranged, demonic. The qualities stressed are those of Nature; it is absorbed in its substance—its physical impact upon the listener through volume and beat, torturing discords, startling shifts in rhythms, key, and extraordinary juxtapositions of material. When a society is integrated, its music *contains* Nature in the Spirit, harmonizes both and begins to represent the Whole. Hesse seems to find Baroque music (Bach is its embodiment) as the best illustration of the character of good music. Baroque gives the widest possible range to the introduction of novelty, variety, surprising combinations of themes, instruments, and forms—all that the disintegrated society expresses. But it integrates, *contains,* these elements through control and order.

That is why a fugue begins the young Knecht on his career. Beginning with a melody that pleases Joseph, the Music Master shows the boy the infinite possibilities of that simple, cherished tune; he adds a voice to the boy's, then surprisingly two voices, then three, then ornaments to embellish the voices, then variations (modifying the melody, the rhythm, and the harmony). Then he relates the four voices by making them respond to one another, support one another, weave about one another, exchange roles, create an intricate network. Having demonstrated the extraordinary complexity potential in the simple melody, the Music Master then creates through the fugue a whole out of this variety. From a fragment of the melody, he abstracts a theme, embodies it in four voices and works them out three times. As he listens to the Music Master's fugue, Joseph is filled with a sense of his calling:

> Behind the music being created in his presence he sensed the world of Mind, the joy-giving harmony of law and freedom, of service and rule. He surrendered himself, and vowed to serve that world and this Master. In those few minutes he saw himself and his life, saw the whole cosmos guided, ordered, and interpreted by the spirit of music (p. 43).

The deepest sense of such music is that beneath its delight or sorrow, beneath its astonishing complexity, is a harmony that makes an affirmation of man and the universe. The Music Master's personality makes clear the nature of this affirmation; although he could inspire fear or sorrow, the keynote of his personality, the ultimate characteristic of Knecht, and the dominant tone of the whole novel is serenity.

The Music Master's serenity is subtle but complicated. Its main characteristics are the deceptive simplicity and peaceful cheerfulness of a Vasudeva or an Abbot Daniel. It is a "radiant cheerfulness" that comes from attunement with the Whole and recognition that true freedom comes from finding one's place within the Whole and working towards it. The work consists of a commitment to discipline of one's self in his vocation to achieve the demands of *the* Self. Thereby, he will create order without and within to transcend the illusory dissonances and incongruities of life. The musician who realizes the true nature of his art does not become lost in its tantalizing beauty (though he does not deny it); he ultimately sees it as an expression of what Hesse believes to be the highest good: unity.

But this unity, though simple in appearance, is not any easier to realize than it is to arrive at it through the pain and horror of dying through the thousand selves. It is the most difficult act that a man can perform. It demands perfect honesty to produce perfect insight and then requires the deepest commitment and the hardest work and self-discipline to make that insight a living reality. As Knecht is to do, the Music Master realizes Self by becoming a perfect master of his vocation, then striving—as a teacher—to make that vocation, that "calling," a reality in the lives of other men such as Joseph, and at the end of his life transcending his vocation to arrive at that which its particular character embodied: the Wholeness of a merged Self and Universe.

In later episodes, the Music Master will stress to Knecht the importance of meditation as a means of keeping aware of the Whole and service as a means of realizing the Whole through the Self. Meditation prevents the vocation from becoming a goal in itself; it releases the worker from the passion of work and places him in a contact with the Whole that restores to his life meaning, harmony, peace, and cheerful serenity. But there are dangers in a life solely devoted to meditation. The meditator may become a mystic, totally out of contact with society and nature. He has an obligation to *himself* to maintain such contact, for as central and important as the Spirit is, it resides in a psyche that responds to society and a body that responds to nature. He may bypass them and obtain a vision of the Whole. But he cannot bypass them and *enter* into the Whole. He must live through the social and the natural experience to attain the complete spiritual experience.

The Music Master believes that the necessary mode of living is service. And his specific mode of service is teaching. The true teacher not only fulfills his social and natural self by his service, but he leads society into recognition of its relationship to the Whole. In short, he best realizes Self by leading the whole of humanity to realize Self. The ultimate goal of everyone is to return to the Whole. The fate of humanity is to begin in innocence within the unrealized Whole, to fall into experience, and to explore and contain the totality of experience to arrive at the realized Whole.

Service, paradoxically, is the route to the greatest freedom. A man is only free to choose what principles he will serve. That choice made, he is in bondage to them. But that servitude will not seem like servitude, for if he has chosen wisely, he has chosen to do exactly what he wishes to do and must do in accordance with the demands of his Self. For instance, Castalia makes the choice for the student on the premise that the teacher knows better than the student his true nature; if the system makes a mistake (as it does in assigning Knecht to the diplomatic corps), it revises itself and seeks again the proper role for the student. In its ideal form, Castalia should be an organic society that is a *harmony of individuals,* rather than a mechanically conceived Establishment annihilating individuals. Each man doing what he himself knows he must do serves the whole of Castalia. He need not limit or compromise himself because a true discovery of Self is a recognition of its identity with the Whole. The greatest freedom is attained through harmony.

As the power and capacity of an individual within the Castalian hierarchy increases, so must his servitude. Here lies one of Knecht's greatest problems, for like the Music Master he is an enormously charismatic personality—charismatic because others intuit in him the universal truth that he perceives and responds to. Such a power with such a basis makes service even more obligatory to Knecht. If he is to rule Castalia and not to destroy it, Knecht must act so that it allows its membership to act as they need to. As Master, Knecht must *contain* Castalia, be responsive to all its infinite human possibilities and the relationship of those to the Whole. He has the power to do so. He must use that power in service. Otherwise, he will destroy Castalia and in so doing destroy his Self.

Castalia would be ideal if it were the total human society. But it isn't. As the Spirit of Castalia, Knecht serves it to realize its Self. But as the Spirit of Humanity Castalia does not serve society to realize its Self. Castalia is like the meditating mystic who has by-passed society and nature. In the symbol of the Glass Bead Game, Castalia can contemplate the beauty and truth of the Whole. But, like the inexperienced mystic, Castalia cannot *be* the Whole. The war and chaos stemming from the nature of the society that Castalia has not integrated will destroy it.

Simply, Castalia is premature in its withdrawal. The Music Master is not. While keeping in contact with the Whole by regular meditation, he serves others, himself, and his vocation until he has exhausted his nature in action, as Goldmund did. Then nature combines with spirit and the Music Master attains the Whole. At the moment of his death, every part and motion of his body represents music to Knecht. Moreover, the Music Master's face has the cheerful serenity of one who has attained the Whole. Knecht too will attain that cheerful serenity. But his body will be destroyed. The Game has not used it.

My discussion of the Glass Bead Game and music establishes a major issue in the novel: the Game's dangerous lack of relevance to nature and society in contrast to the relevance of music. As I have pointed out, such irrelevance owes much to the human factor. In strong reaction to the twentieth century's devaluation of the intellect, the Castalian hierarchy has emphasized the preservation of culture above its educational function. Whereas the twentieth century had debased truth by popularization, the twenty-fourth has overreacted by purifying it into a Glass Bead Game quite beyond the comprehension of all but a handful of elite intellectuals who have considerable influence in establishing the values of the whole educational system; the purest intellects receive the highest rewards while the coarser ones are ejected into society to teach. It will take Knecht his whole student career to fully realize the danger in this position.

But there is a deeper question that plagues him from the beginning. Is the Game simply a "game" or does it have the broader dimension of music? It is a difficult question to answer, for again the human factor enters. There are musicians like Carlo Ferromonte who maintain a typical Castalian attitude toward their vocations. And then there are men like the Music Master who can take a more balanced approach; he is aware of the relative importance of *both* the beauty and morality of music, he uses meditation to realize the former and teaching to realize the latter. The active moral life giving body to the passive contemplative life, the Music Master ultimately becomes a "saint," the human embodiment of music. Can the Game allow Knecht to do the same, or is it simply an intellectual fad? This is obviously a vital question, for the Game was persistently the focal point at every stage of Castalia's development. Loss of the Game could mean the loss of Castalia. And during Knecht's life the threat is very real: not only has the Game no relevance to a society rapidly moving towards war, but Castalians who are not players often have a deep suspicion of those who are.

Knecht has a more central problem, which the whole issue of the Game emphasizes. Like Siddhartha, Harry and Hermine, Narcissus and Goldmund, Knecht is one of the "special" people: the force of the Self is strong in him. He must discover its dictates and then follow them. This is his "destiny." Will the Self be realized in the Game? Since Knecht will die soon after he leaves the office of Magister Ludi, the answer to that question determines whether or not one believes Hesse's last novel to be a negation of human effort or the same affirmation he has so far made.

There is particular difficulty in establishing Knecht's

state of awareness at any point in the novel. He is both unconsciously and consciously aware of most of what I have suggested so far. But he is not *totally* aware. As I have pointed out in my discussion of the fugue's impact on the adolescent Knecht, his unrealized Self responds quite fully to the congenial external experience through what he will describe as a "call." And the importance of maintaining a proper relationship between meditation and service is made clear by the Music Master to Knecht's conscious mind quite early in the young man's development. But, as Hesse has demonstrated many times, knowledge does not insure wisdom. Knecht has to integrate his ego consciousness with the unconscious Self to realize the latter. So it will not be enough to say that Knecht "knows" something because he has expressed an idea in a letter or symbolized a psychological actuality in a poem or story.

The general movement of Knecht's development is from "call" to "awakening"—from a compelling demand from his unconscious to a conscious awareness of the nature and necessity of that demand. Both words are of great importance in trying to formulate a clear assessment of Knecht's stage of integration. But, unfortunately, we also have the pedantic biographer giving us the facts—and he often omits vital information. Why is Hesse so vague? I think that the ultimate result is that we come to believe that Joseph Knecht is much more omniscient, much more in tune with worlds beyond ours, than Hesse could indicate in any other way.

Here is an outline of Knecht's student years. He receives his "call" from the Music Master, significantly, at the age of puberty. By the time he has left high school (Eschholz), Knecht has already received from the Music Master important lectures on service and meditation. During his university years, he encounters the demands of the active world through his relationship with Plinio Designori; he writes poems expressing a complicated awareness of the virtues and dangers of the Game, and he

160

makes a decision to give the Game a stringent test. This he does in his post-graduate period of "free study." During this period, he displays through his stories, *The Three Lives*, a strong absorption in all of the issues involved, but how much Knecht is aware of the deep significance of his stories is difficult to estimate. He also writes and receives letters that make it clear that he is consciously aware of the nature and value of the Game itself, of his own charismatic power, and of the need to harness that power by service. But knowledge is not enough. It isn't until afterwards, during his instruction in the *I Ching* from Elder Brother, that he first becomes aware that his "awakening" has begun. Then, he gladly accepts an invitation to join the Castalian Order and immediately receives his assignment to the Benedictine monastery, Mariafels.

Although the above summary pretty well presents the main points, there are three subjects that require further commentary: the *Poems*, *The Three Lives*, and the visit with Elder Brother. As I have said, the first two are best read with the student years, for they offer insights and subjective coloring that Knecht's biographer is not able to provide.

During the period of Knecht's introduction to the Glass Bead Game and the opposing world of Plinio Designori, he writes thirteen poems which reveal him progressively coming to terms with the issues of impermanence, nature, society, and the spirit. The poems are important in that they show him much more aware of his field of choices than the biographer can know, and they make it clear that his commitment to the Game is made with the intuition that it will pass. Yet he does make that commitment, for the Game best embodies for his specific age the perception of the Whole. Unlike the Music Master, Knecht is destined to represent the twenty-fourth century to itself.

In the first poem, Knecht is frightened; like Goldmund he sees that the world is transitory and he yearns to "stiffen into stone, to persevere" (p. 397). With little of Harry Haller's anxiety, he rejects the solution of becoming a one-dimensional man: "Let us strike one dimension off our list" (p. 398). He has a powerful recognition of the demands of the mother-world upon him, a fact which the biographer virtually ignores and one which re-emerges as significant in "The Legend." Knecht has little doubt about the power upon the most "tranquil" Game-players of "blood, barbarity, night . . . begetting, birth, and suffering, and death" (p. 399). The most primitive of men could intuit the players' unconscious obsession by "love of life and death, or lust and anguish . . . twins whom no one can distinguish" (p. 400).

Turning from the players to the Game itself, Knecht has the same perception that Goldmund obtained about art; above the transitory mother-world, man's spirit can rise and win, "by longing, immortality" (p. 401). But can the Game do so? Knecht has a vision of the last Glass Bead Game player playing his game futilely in a world depopulated by war and disease; his Game will not forestall such destruction. But then there is Bach: out of night and chaos, a Bach toccata creates an entirely new and beautiful universe, implicitly replacing the one lost by the last player. Yet will that world endure? No. "A Dream" of a library of astonishing books containing fantastic truths is visited by an ancient librarian who erases these new toccata-worlds as soon as they appear; the finest productions of human culture are as transitory as the men who made them.

Yet somewhere there is the truth, the way, the Whole. If the Game will not be the answer to society's problems, yet its players can preserve "in metaphor and symbol and in psalm" the lost knowledge and experience of the Whole (p. 407). That is the power of each human being: the ancient scholar embodying his wisdom in his final book, the young scholar introducing new insights in his first book, the boy blowing bubbles in water—each are living in the transitory, illusory world (Maya), but "in each of them the Light of Eternity sees its reflection, and burns more joyfully" (p. 408). And from time to time in the history of humanity a certain man in a certain civilization can rediscover the ancient truths; others in a more degenerate civilization—and again Knecht stresses the point—can preserve the light for better civilizations.

Knecht concludes with what is to become his favorite poem, "Stages," which he originally calls "Transcend!"; his Castalian sophistication prevents him from using the final title until he regains the insights with which he closes his career. Here, he realizes that each man's truths will fade away, that when that moment comes each man should be willing to bid farewell to that truth—no matter how beautiful it was—and that beyond all such specific truths is the "Cosmic Spirit" pressing man "stage by stage . . . to fresh and newer spaces" (p. 411). He concludes the *Poems* with a commitment to the Glass Bead Game in full knowledge that it will pass as will all the productions of man. But it is the finest production of his age, the strongest master, for it best represents to the twenty-fourth century the truth of the Whole:

> And when we tell our beads, we serve the whole,
> And cannot be dislodged or misdirected,
> Held in the orbit of the Cosmic Soul (p. 412).

Presumably after he has written these poems, Knecht wins Plinio Designori's deep respect for himself and for the Castalian ideal. But Plinio has also won Knecht's respect for his position. The musician Carlo Ferromonte concludes:

> The contrast of world and Mind, or of Plinio and Joseph, had before my eyes been transfigured from the conflict of two irreconcilable principles into a double concerto (p. 94).

But although the relationship of "world and Mind" has been established, their unification will remain a problem with Knecht until his death.

Written shortly afterwards, *The Three Lives* present many more difficulties than do the *Poems*. Whereas the latter contain explicit statements about Knecht's beliefs, the former are totally symbolic. A second difficulty is that Hesse's location of the *Lives* at the end of the book suggests that, along with the *Poems*, they are in some way an explanation of Knecht's puzzlingly sudden death. I will treat the *Lives* twice, here and again at the end of the chapter. I will try now to determine to what extent they allow Knecht to solve his problems during his student years.

Before he wrote the *Lives*, Knecht had had a second "call" through which he had a vision of the relationship of the Game to the Whole. But his mood is mixed: his controversy with Plinio has aroused doubts about the value of his contemplated vocation; the doubts are so deep and the trauma so great that he has withdrawn from student society. During this period of withdrawal, he tests the Game's mechanics and is satisfied, but is doubtful if he can make it a vocation; it stimulates his mystic propensities too much. Finally, he visits the recluse Elder Brother for instruction in the *I Ching*. At that moment, he makes "the beginning of his awakening": although he has decided to come out of his retreat and act, he still doesn't know how he should act. Castalia makes the choice for him: it sends him to Mariafels.

In the light of these conditions, I think that the central conscious relevance these *Lives* would have had to Knecht at the time had to do with the relationship of world and Mind, specifically in terms of what form of action Mind can take that will relate it to world. The most persistent active character in the *Lives* is the teacher. But in light of the fact that in this period, "Knecht felt hardly drawn to such work" (p. 121), he couldn't have seen in the *Lives* at this moment what he will finally discover; he is to be a schoolmaster. It is more likely that now he sees himself as student—the preserver of the Whole rather than Its communicator. This theory is supported by the fact that although he is a teacher as well as a student in the first story, he is only a student in the second and third stories. Furthermore, the stories progress from one of a teacher-student who is deeply involved in the world to one who is a monk to one who lives through the world only to reject it entirely. Consciously, Knecht must have regarded the last "Life" as most congenial, for he too has withdrawn from society to contemplate the Whole through the Glass Bead Game. But, of course, the *Lives* mean much more to Knecht than he "knows"; at this moment, the Self is sending out very strong signals of its nature which are not penetrating his conscious—largely because at this moment he has only had the experience of being a student, not of being an active agent in the world.

In "The Rainmaker" Knecht lives in a neolithic matriarchal tribe, the only significant male member of which is the rainmaker who serves the tribal society by giving it guidance in its vital agricultural activities. He is not a charlatan; his advice comes from hard-learned knowledge of subtle natural phenomena and a deep wisdom through which he is attuned to nature and the Whole. The old rainmaker Tutu selects Knecht as the man to succeed him and teaches him his arduously learned skills. Knecht improves upon them and gradually begins to see the role of the male as distinct from the matriarchs and uniquely important to the survival of the tribe. Eventually, nature and the matriarchs combine to destroy him, as is the way of the mother-world; he voluntarily sacrifices himself. But he makes certain that his office goes to his own son Tutu, whom he has preserved from the traumatizing knowledge of the natural disaster that destroyed him and to whom he has passed on the old Tutu's now-enriched knowledge and wisdom. There is not a simple transmission of knowledge here, but a positive evolution towards greater and greater perception of the Whole.

"The Father Confessor" takes place in the fourth century, A.D., during the founding of the monasteries by St. Hilarion. This story dramatizes the student-teacher relationship of two of the desert hermits to whom people would go for spiritual comfort. The youngest of the two fathers is Josephus Famulus (again "servant" or *knecht*). His method of cure is like that of a modern psychotherapist: he passively listens, and then he forgives. His older counterpart, Dion Pugil (the "fighter"), takes stern and sometimes violent action against his patients; often intuiting their problems before they speak and piercing their evasions, he gives strong advice and rigid penances. Plagued by a Siddharthean spiritual nausea, the passive Famulus eventually seeks to be cured himself by the active Dion. He encounters the old man in an oasis, makes his confession to him, and to his surprise receives the same response that he himself would have given. Dion takes Famulus home with him, teaches him greater compassion for the non-Christian and the criminal, and imposes upon him the penance of becoming his servant. When the old man knows that he is to die, he tells Famulus that on the day they first met, he had been travelling to receive solace from Famulus. But Famulus had asked first, and Dion had sacrificed his spiritual quiet to arouse the same in the other; the teacher had served the student while the student served the teacher. At Dion's request, Famulus plants a tree upon Dion's grave "and lived to see the year in which the tree bore its first fruit" (p. 483). The tree, of course, implies as it did in *Narcissus and Goldmund* that there has been a unification of Famulus' passivity with Dion's activity, something of the nature of that synthesis which Knecht seeks with Plinio Designori. Again, the student is enriched and carries mankind further toward the perception of the Whole.

In "The Indian Life" Knecht now becomes Dasa, of noble birth but exiled because of the jealousy of his stepmother. A shepherd, he visits the city of his step-brother, King Nala, enjoys a festival there, marries the beautiful Pravati whom he encounters upon his return, and loses her to Nala. He assassinates Nala and flees to the jungle where he had earlier encountered an ancient holy man, a yogi. He lives with the yogi—serving him by bringing him food and drink. But, like the guru Vasudeva in *Siddhartha,* the teacher does little explicit teaching: the yogi is rapt in his vision of the Whole; Dasa watches him meditate and tries to imitate him. When Dasa beseeches him for instruction, the yogi merely laughs and says, "Maya" (the illusion that leads us to believe in the world of objects and events). When Dasa begs for instruction in Maya, the yogi gives him a gourd to fetch some water.

At the spring, Dasa unwittingly enters into Maya: he regains Pravati, his lost throne, and a son; he enters into conflict with his wife and into war with a neighboring prince, is defeated and loses both son and wife. He awakens again by the stream. Having lived through the ecstasy and terror of life, he understands as does Knecht that it is an illusion; the only reality is that of the Whole in which the holy man exists. Conveying his desire only by a "look which contained a trace of benevolent sympathy," the yogi accepts the shepherd-king as disciple. Dasa withdraws; he "never again left the forest" (p. 520).

The student Knecht's final vision is presumably that of Dasa. As Dasa's dream embodied Maya, so does the Game embody the transitory cultural achievements of past civilizations, preserve them, and relate them in a harmony that, when seen "with a truly meditative mind," symbolizes:

> the interior of the cosmic mystery, where in the alteration between inhaling and exhaling, between heaven and earth, between Yin and Yang, holiness is forever being created (p. 105).

167

Its embodiment of both Maya *and* the Whole of human truths makes it "truly a *lingua sacra,* a sacred and divine language" to which he will commit himself (p. 105).

Realizing the value of the Game, Knecht still sees a danger within it, which he confides to the Music Master; he fears that he cannot make the Game his vocation, for the ecstatic vision of the Whole will lead him to renounce the world as Maya. The Master replies that the Whole cannot be taught (any more than the yogi "taught" Dasa), no matter what its embodiment: the Game, music, or poetry. One learns only through the difficult experience that Knecht shared with Dasa. The role of the teacher is to serve by making Game, music, or poem accessible to the student:

> The task of the teacher and scholar is to study means, cultivate tradition, and preserve the purity of methods (p. 108).

It is then up to the student himself to perceive the Whole in that which he has been taught. As for Knecht's losing himself in the Whole, the Master wryly comments: "A Game Master or teacher who was primarily concerned with being close enough to the 'innermost meaning' would be a very bad teacher" (p. 107).

Knecht still has to decide whether to continue his withdrawal or to act in the Order. He comes to a decision through his visit to Elder Brother, a decision which he describes as his first moment of "awakening"—the emergence into consciousness of the hitherto unconscious "call." Here he has a double insight. The first is that the oracular *I Ching* to which Elder Brother has devoted himself is a symbolic system that gives guidance to humanity—in contrast to the Glass Bead Game. When Knecht naively proposes to Elder Brother that he wants to incorporate the *I Ching* into the Glass Bead Game, Elder Brother laughs:

"Anyone can create a pretty little bamboo garden in the world. But I doubt that the gardener would succeed in incorporating the world in his bamboo grove" (p. 117).

Presumably, the "pretty little bamboo garden" is the Glass Bead Game, about which Knecht's first recorded observation is:

> The whole of both physical and mental life is a dynamic phenomenon, of which the Glass Bead Game basically comprehends only the aesthetic side, and does so predominantly as an image of rhythmic processes (p. 95).

The Game contains only the beauty of the Whole in terms of the cyclic processes of the birth and decay of human mental life. But the *I Ching* represents the Whole. And it uses only two symbols: ——— and — —.

The *I Ching* is fascinating—and disturbing. The first time I used the divining sticks to check Hesse's accuracy, I obtained exactly the same hexagram that he did, out of sixty-four possibilities; Hesse, by the way, was quite accurate. The hexagram that Knecht saw looked like this:

The top three lines represent the mountain, "Gen." The bottom three lines represent the water, "Kan." The whole hexagram represents "youthful folly" in the terms by which Elder Brother describes it. But there is much more in this oracle than he makes evident. In discussing the "Kan" hexagram (formed when the top three lines as

169

well as the bottom three are "Kan"), Jung suggests some of the psychological implications of the *I Ching:*

> K'an is definitely one of the less agreeable hexagrams. It describes a situation in which the subject seems in grave danger of being caught in all sorts of pitfalls. I have found that K'an often turned up with patients who were too much under the sway of the unconscious (water) and hence threatened with the possible occurrence of psychotic phenomena.[5]

For the moment, I will simply observe that Knecht will die because of a "foolish youth"; and he will drown in a lake at the foot of a mountain. But mountain, lake, and youth all have further symbolic significance, as suggested by Jung's interpretation: they refer to the structure of the psyche and, beyond that, to the nature of the cosmos, the Whole. In contrast to the *I Ching's* astonishingly wide reference, the Glass Bead Game is indeed a "pretty little bamboo garden."

But Elder Brother's garden metaphor is one that can be taken another way—and apparently Knecht chooses that meaning. Elder Brother himself lives in a pretty garden. He can make a garden in the world, but how can he bring the world into the garden? Knecht rejects the role of the gardener. He will not practice the *I Ching* as an isolated eccentric. His qualities of "strength, . . . independence, . . . self-reliance" demand that "he serve only the highest master"(p. 120). That master is the Game. But Knecht's qualities have charismatic impact upon those about him. Obviously, to realize the Self's charisma he must live in the world, not in the Garden. But how is he to use his power upon others? History has shown him that power corrupts the powerful and destroys the weak when it is used as an end. Then he must serve others with his power. But, again, how? The only role available to him in Castalia is teaching—and at this point of his life, he still prefers the Game, despite the doubts that the *I Ching* has induced in him.

Castalia takes the choice out of his hands; it accepts him into the order and assigns him to Mariafels. As with the appearance of the Music Master at the moment of "call," at the moment of "awakening" an external development meets a need of the Self. The need for action established, the necessary experience will soon make itself available.

After deciding to join the Castalian Order, Knecht turns his back upon the temptations of Elder Brother's contemplative life and enters into a life of action. This life has three phases: diplomatic service at Mariafels, service as Magister Ludi, and service of society as symbolized by the Designori family. The chapters dealing with Knecht's decision in favor of a life of action are much clearer than others in *Magister Ludi* because Knecht is becoming more consciously aware of his position and because his active life implies that he articulate that position much more clearly. While Knecht means "servant," Joseph means "increase"; he will now begin the second function.

While Castalia's covert motive for sending Knecht into the Benedictine monastery at Mariafels is to achieve a diplomatic alliance between itself and the Catholic Church and thereby begin to unite the institutionalized spiritual interests of the country, Knecht's explicit assignment is to teach the Glass Bead Game to Benedictine monks. In this capacity, he wins one young follower, Anton; otherwise he creates little real interest in the Game. However, he convinces Father Jacobus that there is a possibility of a dialogue between Church and Castalia and thus achieves his true mission.

But his relationship with Jacobus is more that of student than of teacher. The old historian conveys to Knecht the necessity of an institution's historical self-awareness. As the historian, Jacob Burckhardt (upon whom Father Jacobus is modelled), once said: "Historical knowledge does not make us shrewder for the next time, but wiser forever."[6] The Castalian focus on eternal truth leads to knowledge but not to wisdom. Forgetful of its origins and lodged in the timeless, Castalia will not attain the full development that comes only through the embodiment of knowledge in experience.

The Church has such wisdom, for it is an institution which has lived in the world as well as beyond it. The history of Mariafels suggests the mode in which this wisdom developed. It began as an institution stressing theology and logic as Castalia had stressed the symbolic organization of the philosophical content of its disciplines. But the concern was not sustaining; Mariafels became dormant. Then it moved from absorption in the intellect to a somewhat Castalian absorption in beauty; it became a great music center. This seems to be the stage at which Castalia is at the time of *Magister Ludi;* it contemplates the beauty of Mind rather than the spiritual significance which had first absorbed it. But Mariafel's service of God rather than abstract Truth has taken it further. Mariafels has moved on to a role which Castalia is just beginning to think about; in a chaotic society, it has become a political force, "a little island of rationality where the better minds among the opposed parties . . . groped their way toward reconciliation" (p. 138). Its last great achievement was to arrange a peace treaty among "the exhausted nations" (p. 138). Now Mariafels is simply marking time to see what the new developments will be. It will survive them, for it has learned the lesson of the historian: "To study history means submitting to chaos and nevertheless retaining faith in order and meaning . . . a very serious task . . . and possibly a tragic one" (p. 151.). These words of Father Jacobus are ominous for Knecht.

Although much attracted by Mariafels, Knecht knows that for him there is no possibility of conversion, nor of an active role as a politician. Clearly, he is in the same state of development as Castalia. Jacobus observes that both Knecht and Castalia are far from attaining the faith that Mariafels embodies. Before becoming political, the Castalians must achieve knowledge of man: "in his besti-

172

ality and as the image of God" (p. 170). All they know is the nature of Castalians, "a rare experiment in breeding" (p. 170). Knecht agrees with Jacobus that he must serve "the system of which he was a member, without asking whether it could claim perpetual existence, or even a long span of life" (p. 156).

Knecht returns to Castalia to be a student of the Glass Bead Game, and he wins a major competition. But, as usual, the external world is not long in calling him; he becomes elected Magister Ludi upon the sudden death of Thomas von der Trave. The days before the election offer a significant prophesy of Knecht's fate. A man who regards the Game as "akin to art," rather than religion or philosophy, the aristocratic Master Thomas' last Game is a failure, a suggestion that the aesthetic absorption of Castalia is coming to an end and that it senses a new need, as is suggested by its gropings toward the Church. But endings demand sacrifice. Master Thomas' assistant, the "Shadow" Bertram, is brutally forced by the Castalian elite into a position that results in his suicide; the younger elite's long-continuing aversion toward him symbolizes a reaction against the implicit, negative aspects of Master Thomas' aesthetic rule. But this reaction is far from the Castalian conscious—thus its brutality. Castalia will not sacrifice Knecht; he will sacrifice himself to bring it into deeper awareness of its human reality as symbolized by its savage act. When Knecht receives the appointment as Magister Ludi, he feels "as if he himself were now on the point of sacrificing and extinguishing himself like the Shadow" (p. 198).

But Knecht masters his job as few, if any, Magisters had ever done. His first and most exhausting act is to employ his charismatic power to win over the younger Castalian elite, who, like the radical aesthete Tegularius, had forced the destruction of Bertram. This he accomplishes very well, welding together a body of young men from whom the future Castalian leaders will be recruited. Some of these students will later write "The Legend." Knecht has taken his first step toward the role of teacher.

For him, this period is a second stage in his "awakening." But it is "cooling and sobering" (p. 209); his astonishing achievements have left him strangely unmoved.

In a lecture to young teachers, Knecht summarizes his past conclusions: the Game demands stringent intellectual discipline but also an awareness of its necessary flexability as a discipline which unites the others and saves them from the dangers of specialization; the teachers of the Game are most vital in attaining these ends and keeping the Game in a constant state of development; the greatest obligation of the teacher is to avoid "empty virtuosity" and power-seeking by keeping in balance the two principles of Castalia: "objectivity and love of truth in study, and . . . the cultivation of meditative wisdom and harmony" (pp. 216-17). He urges the young Castalian teachers to add to their intellectual education one in "the morality of the Order" and learn to progress by moving back and forth between the active life and the contemplative life, allowing each to fortify the other. Joseph the Increaser begins to realize that Magister Ludi means not only "Master of the Game" but originally had meant "schoolmaster" too.

Time must pass before Knecht fully realizes his next course of action. His immediate task is to address himself to the renovation of the Game, which he does by creating a "psychological" Game (one involving meditation upon the significance of the Whole that the Game represents): the Chinese House Game. Although the exact nature of this Game is, as always, obscure, it symbolizes Knecht's desire to somehow relate the Game to the life external to Castalia. He draws upon China once more to obtain the proper symbols, and makes the Game literally into a house within society and universe. His studies of the *I Ching* had led him to knowledge of the "ancient ritual Confucian pattern" for building a house by so arranging its gates, walls, buildings and courtyards as to make its actual physical location a "symbol of the cosmos and of man's place in the universe" (p. 224). He has tried to suggest the humanity of the Game without sacri-

ficing its universality. The impact of Kn[...]
the outside world as well as Castalia is [...]
the world remains unchanged.

The period as Magister is not only a time for [...]
achievements. He continues to have insights as wel[...]
of the most important of these comes through his witne[...]
ing the death of his old teacher, the Music Master, the
man

> whose look and example hovered over Joseph's
> life and who would always be a generation and
> several stages of life ahead of him . . . would
> always remain his patron and model, gently
> compelling him to walk in his steps (p. 200).

The new stage is one that Knecht will never explicitly
express as the one he seeks: canonization. After a life of
healthily related action and contemplation, the Music
Master is finally prepared for the immersion in the Whole
that until the completion of his life could have been such
a dangerous course. The nature of that completed Self-
realization is so important to an understanding of Knecht's
death that I must quote Knecht's lengthy sentence upon
it in its entirety. Note particularly the transformation of
the body:

> It was as if by becoming a musician and Music
> Master he had chosen music as one of the ways
> toward man's highest goal, inner freedom, pur-
> ity, perfection, and as though ever since making
> that choice he had done nothing but let himself
> be more and more permeated, transformed, puri-
> fied by music—his entire self from his nimble,
> clever pianist's hands and his vast, well-stocked
> musician's memory, to his pulses and breathing,
> to his sleep and dreaming—so that he was now
> only a symbol, or rather a manifestation, a per-
> sonification of music (p. 239).

175

ection come from submitting
ctual, and physical being to a
ner and theorist.

mes Music itself: his personal
ed observer is of "an altogether
c which absorbs everyone who
a song for many voices absorbs
239). It is the highest goal of
echt significantly observes, avail-
er than music, such as those of
nguist, and—although he doesn't
say so—eve_   r of the Game. Knecht has become
Master of the Game by being its servant; he has submitted
himself to its teachers, its discipline, and the Castalian
hierarchy that embodies it. Through this service, he has
become so intimately aware of the nature of the Game,
that he realizes that it seeks through him a greater dimension than it has ever yet attained: the human dimension. The master and servant of the Game is ready to
become the schoolmaster—and servant—of society.

While perfectly supervising the administration of Castalia, Knecht gradually enters into another "awakening";
he begins to see the necessity of the "schoolmaster" to
Castalia. Again, the external world coincides with the internal world; an emergent internal reality will soon find
its correspondence in the external world, for what that
infinitely complex world doesn't offer us is simply that
which we can't see. Knecht first begins to see the desira-
bility of teaching when he makes a reality of the charisma that characterizes the becoming Self. Before he had
taught, he knew that he could do it well, but he wanted
to study the Game. But then in Mariafels he taught the
young Anton and aged Jacobus, and in Castalia he taught
the young elite teachers; upon the death of the Music
Master, he led young Petrus back from a deranged absorption in the Whole into an active life. Throughout,
Knecht has felt a deep attraction for the non-Castalians

and the natural life they represent. As a child, he wa.
shocked at the dismissal of other Eschholz boys; it meant
to him both the power of the outside world and the inability of Castalia to cope with that power. From his
debates with Designori and Father Jacobus, he not only
won acceptance for Castalia and the Bead Game, but also
gained insight into the power and validity of the worlds
of society and of faith. The teacher is at the same time
the student. He must learn the student's nature and needs
to communicate his own; to teach another well is to
strengthen, enrich, and thereby realize one's Self.

There lies the salvation of Castalia. Emphasis on the
schoolmaster's role will strengthen it doubly; it will protect itself against the world by leading the world to understand the value of Castalia—its Truth, not its Game—
and it will lead Castalia to a full spiritual development
by integrating the world's experience with its knowledge.
When he looks at his friend Tegularius, Knecht sees how
sorely Castalia needs such a marriage of its Truth to the
world's nature. He sees in the radical and unstable young
genius "two things in one: embodiment of the finest
gifts to be found in Castalia, and at the same time a por-
tent of the demoralization and downfall of those abilities"
(p. 249). Castalia is clearly "degenerating from senility
and from relaxation of the meditative morality of the
Order . . . . this highly developed freely roaming intellectual culture no longer had any goals beyond egotistic
enjoyment of its own overbred faculties" (p. 249). To
save such men as Tegularius, the "great educator" Knecht
relies fundamentally on nature rather than intellect; he
uses Tegularius' "love and admiration" for him. But that
love and admiration come to Knecht because of his own
honesty to Self which produces in him the charismatic
"harmonious personality" by which the Music Master be-
witched his students. Whether or not he knows it, each
man aspires to the Whole through realization of the Self;
the man among them closest to that goal has the impact
upon them of the Whole itself. Like Dasa's yogi, his radiant presence will make visible to aware disciples the

beauty of the Whole. In this sense, Christ and
ch was a Schoolmaster.
: perception is a further stage of Knecht's
." In a contest between Self and Castalia,
t choose Self. The importance of Castalia and
its Game lay only in their ability to lead Knecht to realization of the Whole through realization of the Self. If
Castalia should part from the route to the Whole, Knecht
must part from Castalia. It is not an easy decision. For
Knecht is the heart of the present Castalia—the embodiment of the Game, just as the Music Master was the embodiment of music. In his conversations with Designori,
Knecht bears the mark of the saint: cheerful serenity. As
Knecht tells Plinio toward the end of his career as Master
of the Game:

> "Such cheerfulness is neither frivolity nor com-
> placency; it is supreme insight and love, affirma-
> tion of all reality, alertness on the brink of all
> depths and abysses; it is a virtue of saints and
> of knights; it is indestructible and only increases
> with age and nearness to death. It is the secret
> of beauty and the real substance of art" (p. 291).

And it is just through the Game that he has obtained this
cheerful serenity:

> "Our Glass Bead Game combines all three prin-
> ciples: learning, veneration of the beautiful, and
> meditation; and therefore a proper Glass Bead
> Game player ought to be drenched in cheerful-
> ness as a ripe fruit is drenched in its sweet juices"
> (p. 292).

But the arrival of cheerful serenity signals "nearness to
death."

Knecht's reasons for leaving Castalia are multiple and
complex, but they cohere. The most obvious personal
reason is that the tragedy of Designori's life and family

as well as that threatening his son is a signal failure of Castalia to respond to the needs of society. In his "Circular Letter" Knecht elaborates upon the point. Internal dangers to Castalia are its intellectual snobbery and its parochial ignorance of the world's values and drawbacks. This ignorance is exemplified by Castalia's contempt for the subject of history; one important lesson yet to be learned is that the nature of the Whole manifests itself through cycles of destruction and creation as it manifests itself alternately through Nature and Mind. Such a period of destruction will sweep Castalia away, for the society that it did not serve now prepares for war:

> Then scholars and scholarship, Latin and mathematics, education and culture, will be considered worth their salt only to the extent that they can serve the ends of war (p. 329).

What can Castalia do about it? The Castalian would be an inept ruler, so he should not seek power. As a politician, he would compromise his nature, which is adherence to the Truth for the preservation of society—its very technology and science rests upon that foundation. To lose it would be to return to the cave. Beyond that, the intellectual who sacrifices truth to the power world of the politicians and the generals "becomes intensely diabolical . . . far worse than instinctual bestiality, which always retains something of the innocence of nature" (p. 332). The duty of Castalia then is to Truth: "If need be, he must sacrifice his person, but never his fealty to the life of the mind" (p. 332).

But for the Game—it is irrevocably lost. Although Knecht is Magister Ludi, he does not believe that Castalia's action should be to save the Game. The most beautiful but the most impractical element of Castalia, the Game will be the first thing to go when war comes. But Castalia *must* preserve Truth. And the only way to do that is to exchange the Master of the Game for the Schoolmaster; Knecht urges Castalia to send "its brave

179

and good schoolmasters" out to the people. The elite schools will topple after the Game goes, but they must preserve Truth by staffing

> the secular schools on the outside where burghers and peasants, artisans and soldiers, politicians, military officers, and rulers are educated and shaped while they are still malleable children. That is where the basis for the cultural life of the country is to be found, not in the seminars or in the Glass Bead Game (pp. 334-5).

At last Knecht is fully "awakened"—as a Castalian. He reviews his life and understands now that the Self "that had brought him to Waldzell, to Mariafels, into the Order, into the office of Magister Ludi, was now leading him out again" (p. 350). He realizes that the life of action that he chose in those past existences is now leading him out into the world itself to a new, unknown destiny, and that ultimately "for unknown reasons he was by nature more inclined to action than acquiring knowledge, that he was more instinctual than intellectual" (p. 351). He would have been able to remain in Castalia had it been "the world, the whole multifarious but indivisible world, instead of being merely a tiny world within the greater, or a section boldly and violently carved out of it" (p. 349). But it isn't. And so he must bid farewell to Castalia. Finally, Knecht must transcend the life of Magister Ludi as he has the others.

At the moment of his departure from Castalia, Knecht goes to President Alexander to resign his office. The debate is important; it is a struggle for the Game itself. As representative of the valuable meditative life, Alexander presents to Knecht the duty that he owes Castalia. But Knecht replies that he owes a higher duty to himself, to the Whole. He joined Castalia because, like St. Christopher, he can serve only the "strongest master," and an active existence in the world is now the strongest. He has not betrayed Castalia; in fact, he would betray it were he to stay in disobedience to the dictates of Self striving towards the Whole. Alexander is skeptical about these dictates and suggests that they are illusory "revelations from higher powers, communications or summons from the realm of an objective, eternal, or divine truth" (p. 365). But Knecht maintains that the Whole is a very basic reality in the psyche and denies perceiving it in any other terms. Each awakening has caused a painful reaction; even if, at the moment, he did not understand what was happening, he would soon understand and would become "awake and clearheaded and receptive" (p. 366). More important, history reveals that this moment of necessity comes to cultures as well as individuals, and nothing will forestall it. The individual life and the group life are both a series of lives and deaths, ever transcending one another, ever moving ahead to new beginnings. And in Knecht right now this new beginning is the full realization of his love for the world, a love that began with Father Jacobus' imparting the vastness and richness of ever-changing society and nature; a love that was nourished by his finding increasing joy in teaching "younger and younger pupils"; that was completed and realized by the entry of it into his life in the person of Plinio Designori. He concludes that he has worked so hard to persuade Alexander because to transcend Castalia is not to forsake it but to lead it past its dangerous present. He wishes Castalia to value him for what he has given it, to understand the truth and necessity of his decision, and to work for it "on the outside" (p. 373). Alexander refuses to acknowledge the justice of Knecht's step but accepts his resignation. Yet when the schoolmaster leaves, the President becomes a human again: as incomprehensible as Knecht is, "he had loved this man" even his "way of walking,"

a firm, rhythmic step that was also light, almost airy, expressing something between dignity and childlikeness, between priestliness and the dance —a strange, lovable, and elegant walk. . . . It ac-

corded . . . with his peculiar way of being a
Castalian and Magister, his kind of mastership
and serenity, which sometimes reminded Alexander of the aristocratically measured manner of
his predecessor, Master Thomas, sometimes of
the simple, heartwarming former Music Master
(p. 375).

Alexander thinks that he is losing a beautiful and beloved
friend. But he is losing the Game itself. The Age of Castalia is coming to an end. The Age of the Schoolmaster
is beginning.

Knecht's death has caused great disagreement among
Hesse critics:

It is certainly true that over few episodes within
the corpus of modern German literature has
there been so much controversy . . . as there
has been over the ending of *The Glass Bead
Game*.[7]

Such controversies do not indicate that the critics are
fools or that the artist is incompetent but that he has
constructed an experience in which each reader can find
himself; in my opinion, the ambiguity of the ending of
Magister Ludi is a certain sign of the highest art. It is a
symptom of universality, of an approach to the Whole
in which each different and individual man finds himself
contained. To some, Knecht's death is a failure—either
on Knecht's part or on Hermann Hesse's. Hesse himself
was aware of the multiplicity of interpretations his ending
invites and chose (not dictated) the one that pleased him
most:

Knecht's death can naturally have many interpretations. For me the central one is that of sacrifice, which he valiantly and joyfully fulfills. The

way I intend it he has not thereby broken off his task of educating the youth, he has fulfilled it.[8]

The point that I have been working towards throughout this chapter is that as the human embodiment of the Glass Bead Game Knecht must die. I do not suggest that he is "aware" that he will drown that beautiful day in Belpunt (the "beautiful bridge"). But he has had many intimations of disaster from the martyrdom of Bertram and his own depression at receiving the magistracy, from his growing "cheerful serenity" so symptomatic of nearing death, from his constant descriptions of the evolution of Self as a cycle of births and deaths, and from his expression to Alexander of a craving for "risk, difficulty, and danger . . . deprivations and suffering" (p. 362).

> If only he had been able to clarify to Master Alexander what seemed so clear to him; if only he had been able to prove that the apparent willfulness of his present action was in reality service and obedience, that he was moving not toward freedom, but toward new, strange, and hitherto unknown ties; that he was not a fugitive, but a man responding to a summons; not headstrong, but obedient; not master, but sacrifice! (p. 351).

Certainly, Knecht sees himself as a sacrifice. And though he does not deliberately die when he plunges into the icy water, he knows that he is tired, ill, unused to the mountains and to physical exertion; he makes a clear decision to win young Tito as his student by not "opposing cool, adult rationality to this invitation to a test of strength" (p. 393). But again Knecht receives the "call": "The summons was stronger than the warning, his will stronger than his instinct" (p. 393). This time the call is a call to death and so, in obeying the strongest master, Knecht is destroyed.

I can't regard this conclusion as Hesse's sudden warning not to obey the Self. There are more issues than death involved—and I think they become clearer if the symbolic imagery is observed.

The scene is precisely that prophesied by Elder Brother: mountain, lake, and young fool. As in *Narcissus and Goldmund*, the mountain represents "the idea of meditation, spiritual elevation, and communion of the blessed."[9] Castalia is in mountain country, the land of the father. The lake is, of course, a mother-element. Although it frequently symbolizes the very opposite of the mountain, especially disaster and death, I believe that the lake here carries in addition one of its other meanings, water being the element between earth and air, life and death—the element of transition. Knecht doesn't simply die—he transcends. And *The Three Lives* will present the future history of this transcendence.[10]

But before turning to the *Lives*, I want to comment on Tito, the child for whom Knecht makes his sacrifice. As always, the child carries the significance of the unrealized Self; Knecht can be said to be symbolically sacrificing himsef to the Self-as-child that has always given him its "call." The relationship of Tito to the Self as "worshipper" of the Whole is made by his dance, during which "his outspread arms embraced mountain, lake, and sky"—all of the aspects of the Whole. The dance symbolizes the process of becoming, of transformation, uniting the Whole. Knecht's relationship to the child is suggested by the gait that Alexander loved, which reminded him of the child and the dance. But it also reminds him of their opposites. Knecht is no longer child or student; he is the Old Man, the Self fully realized, coming as a "call" to the Self unrealized in Tito. Simultaneously, he is responding to the last demand of the unrealized Self in himself—the demand to die so that new beginnings can be made.

Now if we return to *Joseph Knecht's Posthumous Writings* they receive another dimension. As a student, Knecht presumably thought that they were lives that had led up to him; he was the student of these tales. But now consider him as the teacher—and note the environments of each of these lives. I believe that the *Lives* represent a cycle of humanity from the primitive matriarchal society of the Rainmaker to the ascetic patriarchal society of the desert father Fabulus (its radical opposite) to the society of Dasa, in which both nature and human (jungle and wife) come into control of the realized and unrealized Self—the yogi and his disciple. This is the peak of human development. But there is a fourth "Life"—Joseph Knecht's—which demonstrates the deterioration of the spiritual harmony represented by the yogi and Dasa. As Knecht observes to Plinio about the Hindus' "cheerful serenity," a serenity obtained by the ancient yogi:

> "The world these myths represent begins divinely, blissfully, radiantly, with a springtime loveliness: the golden age. Then it sickens and degenerates more and more; it grows coarse and subsides into misery; and at the end of four ages, each lower than the others, it is ripe for annihilation. Therefore it is trampled underfoot by a laughing, dancing Siva—but it does not end with that. It begins anew with the smile of dreaming Vishnu whose hands playfully fashion a young, new beautiful shining world" (p. 291).

Knecht's is the fourth age—the age of Harry Haller's Aquarius, the age of the flood which will destroy the old to liberate the new.

As Knecht has died, the Glass Bead Game will die. War will destroy it and much of Castalia, too. Castalia is no longer a civilization that can produce art; it contemplates the art of the past and arranges it into the beautiful rhythms of the Game. It is a distillation of art—a beautiful process but one without material, the *human* material of society and nature. The world has run down again, and will pass.

Finally, Hesse is talking about *us*, not about Castalia.

185

And he is talking about the best of us, as well as the worst of us. The best that we value, the most heroic and valid efforts of the finest men in our Age of Reason, will be destroyed as were other worlds just as admirable: the magic world of the primitive; the civilization of Egypt, Greece, and Rome; the spiritual temple of the Church; and now the square, granite office buildings of the State and the ivory towers of the University. With this withering vision before us, shall we give up or throw ourselves insanely into the dance of death that Goldmund watched? We may. But someone will not. Joseph Knecht. Through him—through the servant, the increaser, the teacher—the new civilization will become enriched by the old as ours was enriched by the old. The Spiral is upwards: towards the Whole.

On a second reading, Knecht's *Poems* comment on the passing of the Game in Knecht, the last Bead Game player. He liked the "farewell" poem so well because he intuited that it was necessary and meaningful for him to die so that ultimately the Universal Castalia that he dreamed of would be born, one that could embody in the Whole of Spirit *and* Nature and the truth and beauty of the Game forever. To serve *that* Game, Knecht must die as *this* Game.

The Three Lives not only end with the death of Knecht; they also begin with that death. But the Spiral is upwards. We should not think of progress as a more efficient technology or even as a keener intellect. We must think of it as Wisdom. These *Lives* become different on second reading; they are enriched by the wisdom gained from experiencing Knecht's life. It is the same old tragic-comic cycle of birth, growth, decay, destruction, and birth again. But *the quality has changed*. And *that* is the Way upwards to the Whole.

Knecht dies in the mother-element of water. And the first world he reappears in, in the *Lives*, is the mother-world. The Rainmaker's teacher and, later, his student are both named Tutu. The name of Designori's son is Tito. And Tito is a primitive—but one who at the lake has wedded in his personality the active nature of his father, Plinio, with the passive nature of his spiritual father, Knecht. It is precisely Knecht's sacrifice that pierces Tito's primitive psyche; Knecht imposes upon the boy a responsibility—the responsibility of a guilt that "would demand much greater things of him than he had ever before demanded of himself" (p. 394).

Thus in "The Rainmaker" we almost feel as if the old Tutu is the Tito who has survived the war-destroyed society of Designori. He has come to terms with the mother-world in which Knecht drowned and passes his wisdom on to the new Knecht (the name hasn't changed as it will—he must grow), who learns that the world of the father is in some ways superior to the world of the mother, which remains passive before destruction and death. Knecht the Rainmaker is brought to the Old Man in much the same way that Harry comes to Pablo through Hermine—through the anima Ada. But she quickly fades into the background; the "call" is more important than nature. Knecht the Rainmaker adds to the teacher's knowledge by distinguishing his spiritual power and nature from that of the mother. Although he dies because of her continuing rule, he passes on the power of the Rainmaker to *his* choice, not to hers—the weak and treacherous Maro. And again he does so, by sacrificing himself to the axe—and again the teacher places the responsibility of guilt upon the student, young Tutu. The "guilt" is the knowledge that one man cherishes his vision of the whole so much that he would die to preserve it in the student.

The triumph of the father over the mother is continued in "The Father Confessor." Although both Famulus and Dion Pugil live in a world which is not literally dominated by nature, Famulus expresses the female nature in his passivity while Dion expresses masculine activity. There was in "The Rainmaker" a subordination of male principle to female principle. Now there is a split between the two; instead of the fertile forest the scene is the arid desert of Narcissus. But

187

again the father-principle takes the initiative. Dion sacrifices himself to Famulus, and Famulus' guilt forces him to wed in himself the passive and active natures, as Knecht was forced to the same wedding by Plinio. And a palm grows in the desert.

In "The Indian Life" the true "fourth" age appears. The palm tree has now become a luxurious jungle, to which Hesse devotes some of his most sensuous prose. But now the jungle does not belong only to the mother. At its center, within it but above it and beyond it, sits the silent yogi, his Self attuned to the Whole. Dasa learns through him that the world is illusory—but he learns that by *living* through the illusion, a process Castalia had denied. In his life, he again encounters the mother in the presence of the beautiful but malign Pravata and he again has a son. But this time the mother wins; he is destroyed and the son dies. There is no Tutu to carry on the wisdom that he has learned through the ecstasy and horror of an infinitely varied existence lived from the lowest level of the shepherd to the highest level of king and scholar.

But the end of Dasa's civilization makes no more difference than the end of Knecht's civilization, no more difference than the end of ours. It is a step towards the Whole. Dasa is not father. He is the student of the yogi. Whereas Plinio's active principle was embodied in Dion Pugil and prevailed over Famulus, now it is embodied in Dasa, who is in turn prevailed over by the yogi, the Old Man, the Whole. And the act of teaching is in the mode of Christ, Buddha, the Music Master, of Joseph Knecht himself to the young Tito: his very existence as a fully realized Human, no matter what his personal fate—a cross or a drowning or a canonization—will illuminate man's way to the Whole. The awakened disciple (which means "pupil") will become the next Old Man, the realized Self.

Beyond all these beings there is one more Old Man. He is as cheerfully serene as his novel and its Old Men. And when asked for the Answer, he will laugh and show you the Maya that all the characters in his novels wrestle with so valiantly, so terribly, and so comically. But if you are discontent and ask for the Way, he will smile Siddhartha's "calm, delicate, impenetrable, perhaps gracious, perhaps mocking, wise, thousand-fold smile." And you will see in it the four lives of Hermann Hesse.

CONCLUSION

The Four Lives of Hermann Hesse

One of the goals of this book is to explain why Hermann Hesse is so much admired by the young. The beginning of an answer emerges from the last few sentences of my chapter on *Magister Ludi*. Carl Jung believed that if a man were to progress far enough in self-realization, his impact upon society would be charismatic. Others would behold in him what their own psyches strove towards and become consoled and delighted and inspired by this great man, this Schoolmaster. I believe that Hermann Hesse is such a man.

The search for self-realization in Hesse's novels begins with *Siddhartha* (1922). Set in the ancient India of Buddha, *Siddhartha* draws on Hindu and Buddhistic mysticism to present in the form of a remarkably clear and beautiful legend the evolution of a young intellectual through experience into spiritual wisdom. It ends with Siddhartha's transcending the self to become one with the universe about him and within him. *Steppenwolf* (1927) dramatically shifts the scene. In a Germany demoralized by World War I and suffering from economic and spiritual bankruptcy, the intellectual Harry Haller struggles from a suicidal paralysis to a reconciliation of the warring elements of his personality by immersing himself in what he believes to be the destructive element. Through reference to Carl Jung's theory of personality, Hesse constructs a novel that is in sharp contrast to *Siddhartha;* its characters are painfully and hilariously realistic, its surrealistic Magic Theater is an utterly fantastic riddle, and the benign smile of Siddhartha becomes the wolfish grin of the black humorist. *Narcissus and Goldmund* (1930) shifts subject, characters, setting and tone still again. It is a powerfully erotic and dramatic novel in which the medieval wood-carver Goldmund transcends the world of life and death that he loves so thoroughly to find a longed-for permanence in art; under the surface of this swiftly-moving novel's unobtrusive symbolic imagery is a universe both savage and magnificent. Again, the hero moves from the intellectual world of his friend Narcissus into the blood, sweat, and sex of human experience, then into a spiritual wisdom that once more affirms the harmony of the universe. Finally, *Magister Ludi* (1943) stringently tests the world of the intellectual that the other heroes have departed. The tone of this novel throughout is a deceptively cheerful serenity that even *Siddhartha* doesn't display. The issues have profound implications for the contemporary intellectual and his chief institution, the university. A full range of human solutions—intellect and institutions, art and mysticism, politics and society—is explored and again transcended. The "schoolmaster" Joseph Knecht becomes the living embodiment of his vocation, the Glass Bead Game, and transcends it into a harmonized relationship with the universe that is so complete and fully-realized that it reduces *Siddhartha* to a virtual schema, a plan that Hesse finally made an actuality only by extending his vision of the individual psyche to encompass the history of the whole species.

Throughout these novels there is a further unifying factor—the personality of Hermann Hesse striving for self-realization through trying to live in his art the solutions that his own life have made attractive. While making an affirmation through following one course of action to its conclusion, Hesse has simultaneous awareness of other courses to be followed. Siddhartha succeeds through meditation and withdrawal. But *Steppenwolf* begins with a Harry Haller who has tried such spiritual discipline and found it lacking. Ultimately, he withdraws also but into the chaos and horror of his own existence to find a necessary complement to all he esteems in himself. Goldmund leaves the spirit and the psyche altogether; he actively lives through his senses, body, and emotions in a violent and beautiful world. Only when he has exhausted his body can he withdraw to transcend it. Joseph Knecht also lives a life of action in the equally intricate and complex world of the intellectual. And only when he has exhausted its potential does he leave it. As varied as the approaches are, the process is the same: Hesse realizes himself by living through each life to its conclusion. He begins with an idea, tests it by experience, follows it to its end without ever losing sight of his ultimate belief in universal harmony. And then he begins with another idea. Each life is enriched by the experience of the former life. Each novel has more dimension. Each solution seems closer to *the* solution.

All through my discussions of Hesse's four major novels I have felt like a man trying to shed light on the sun with a flashlight. In writing this book, I have lived through Hesse's books. I had to. The most important thing Hesse can offer is the experience of himself—from the god's smile of Siddhartha to the grin of Steppenwolf to the laughter of Goldmund back again to the smile, to the cheerful, serene smile of the Old Man. I could learn much through books on Hinduism, Jungianism, esoteric symbolism, and aesthetic philosophy. But these books only helped me with Hesse's language. To get to *him*, I had to get to myself. All of his readers must.

Hesse, in offering the universal experience of his own search for self-hood, obviously has universal appeal. But, to return to the question I began with, why does he seem to have a special appeal for younger readers today? Perhaps the answer lies partly in cultural history. Until fairly recently, the major literary figures of English-speaking countries—those most respected by the Establishment—have been in explicit reaction to Romanticism, particularly as it was transmitted to them by the Victorian period; T. E. Hulme, a significant influence on the young T. S. Eliot, condemned Romanticism, the belief in man's unlimited potential, the humanistic attitude, the "emotional and soft," and self-expression. Although few accepted all of Hulme's value judgments, many joined him in his disapproval of self-expression and with him insisted upon a more disciplined and complex literature, e.g. Eliot, who stated "the more perfect the artist, the more completely separate in him will be the man who suffers and the mind which creates."[1]

Yet of late there seems to be an increasing interest in the kind of Romanticism that Hermann Hesse represents. In evidence is more literature which is confessional, which clearly embodies the man who wrote it—particularly if it is quite clear that that man deeply feels while he writes. Other Romantic attitudes are visible: the relegating of reason to a secondary position in relation to other functions of the psyche, the urge to transcend the individual isolated ego through development of these functions, the attendant rekindling of a religious faith in the wholeness of the universe and its inclusion of each man in its grand process. It becomes easier and easier for me to get my classes to respond to Blake (already elevated into prominence by such diverse counter culture leaders as the Fugs and Allen Ginsberg), Coleridge, Byron, Keats, Shelley, Carlyle, and the Victorian essayists; and at least Wordsworth's ideas stimulate them, if not his poetry.

That Hesse is a Romantic is not as astonishing as it would have been had he written in New York or London; whereas by World War I English Romanticism was in decline, it was not until the end of World War II that German Romanticism followed suit (leaving Hesse in rather bad odor in his own country at the present). There was no major English-speaking Romantic voice during the years between the wars. The translation of Hesse provided one. Hesse's receiving the Nobel Prize in 1947 called attention to that voice. The New Directions paperback publication of *Siddhartha*, the connection of that press with the Beat movement, the interest of elements of that movement in *Siddhartha's* mysticism, the importance of that movement in providing stimulus to aspects of the counter culture, and that counter culture's Romantic character—all of these factors seem to me relevant to Hesse's astonishing prominence through the 1960s and into the 1970s.

But cultural history doesn't explain everything. We have had or still have people like Ferlinghetti, Ginsberg, Corso, Kerouac, Kesey, Brautigan, Tolkien, Vonnegut, the black humorists, Buckminster Fuller, McLuhan, Watts, Laing, Leary, Suzuki; we have underground magazines and newspapers and the *Whole Earth Catalog*. There is plenty to read, God knows. Yet Hesse seems to span virtually all of the writers I've just mentioned: in his attacks against the one-dimensional man that has been strangling us for decades, against the prophets of chaos and doom, against the hyper-rationalism, superorganization and materi l sm of the machine age; in his ability to see the virtues of drugs, dreams, music, and mysticism. Perhaps then it could be his breadth, which is another way of saying once more that Hesse himself is the Old Man. Whatever life the young may be experimenting with, Hesse seems to have been there. SIMS meditators carry *Siddhartha* around in their back pockets. *Steppenwolf* speaks both to the rebel and to the head. *Narcissus and Goldmund* appeals to the dropout. *Magister Ludi* provides critical ammunition to the students in our depersonalized, over-specialized universities.

But beyond the specific starting-point of any younger reader is the goal toward which he aims: freedom—especially freedom to be himself, to do his own thing. There is a hierarchy of goals among human beings. If a man doesn't have food, his overriding desire is to eat. Then comes shelter. Then comes the awareness that there are wolves and savages out there: the need for security. Then comes the desire to belong to the tribe—the conformist urge which we all know so well. Then comes the desire to have power over others; only a few get there. Finally, comes the desire of those who are fully fed, fully warm, and fully free from physical or psychological dangers. These people need self-realization. Individuality is born.

Our technology has given birth to this new human being, the individual. But there aren't many. The enormous courage required to create a new world is rare. And there isn't much useful advice coming from the older and supposedly wiser. They see their world threatened; they still need to belong to someone and have someone belong to them. So they club down and jail the freaks and long-haired bastards.

Is it any wonder that Hesse is popular? Here is a man who lived to the age of eighty-five, started with *Siddhartha* at forty-five and finished with *Magister Ludi* at sixty-six—and yet he was *there* and there all the way, through shame, failure, divorce and loss of family, loss of public esteem and money, political exile, two savage wars that slaughtered relatives and friends, and a depression that starved off many of the rest. Hesse was there, an outsider, a freak. And a disciplined scholar and philosopher and a great writer; and one of the major spiritual guides of his age—and now of ours. In short,

195

to a generation of young men and women lacking orientation in a new and difficult struggle, Hermann Hesse is the Schoolmaster.

But not for all. Hesse doesn't appeal so much to many young political activists. Those who dislike him take more or less the position that Alexander takes toward Knecht; he's a cop-out, a narcissistic mystic, a selfish individualist unconcerned about the economic exploitation driving the poor into brutal misery. He wouldn't help dismantle the State and reconstruct a new one. He sat out World War II snugly in Switzerland; some have even maintained that it was his mentality that prepared that war in the first place.

I want to tell a story about another Old Man I met, one of Hesse's German contemporaries who took the political Way: Augustin Souchy, former leader of the German Libertarian Socialists, the anarchists. But Souchy was no bomb-thrower. He was first arrested during World War I as a pacifist; soldiers hung a sign around his neck labelling him a "Dangerous Criminal." He became a disciple of Gustav Landauer, the pacifist Shakespeare scholar, until his teacher was assassinated by the right wing after the war. Souchy continued, becoming a leader; he spoke, wrote, organized. He led the Libertarian Socialists to a break with communism after a visit with Lenin convinced him that the individual liberty which he, like Hesse, prized could not develop in a totalitarian state. He saw his labor support defect to the Nazi Party. He was significant in the successful anarchist experiment in Barcelona during the Spanish Civil War and then saw that too lost to the fascists. He was imprisoned, escaped, worked in Mexico, Cuba, and in post-war Israeli *kibbutzim*. He had known, often intimately, virtually every major political revolutionary of his day, and presently he was in contact with the young leaders of the new European revolution. Throughout, Souchy had worked for the minimum of governmental control and the maximum of individual human liberty.

But he worked for an economic victory. I told him

that I didn't think that prosperity was the ultimate answer; the American revolutionary movement was being manned from both ends of the economic spectrum, after all. There was a deeper discontent, a desire for self-realization. He replied, "We were naive in those days. You see, we hadn't been through it yet. We thought that when everybody was fed and clothed, then everything would take care of itself. We know better now." He too is a Schoolmaster.

Hesse would probably agree with most of what Massimo Teodori calls Thesis I of the New Left:

> Individual *moral revolt* and a desire for nonconformity in all aspects of existence which relate to life-style, come to assume the significance of freedom and of human (and therefore political) liberation themselves, in a context in which both the economic system and social institutions gradually tend, explicitly or implicitly, to invade and define every aspect of the citizens' lives, restricting the fundamental rights of self-realization, self-expression and control over one's own life.[2]

But Hesse would probably change the phrase, "rights of self-realization," to "duty of self-realization." And he would certainly reject the crucial parenthesis, "(and therefore political)." But let him speak for himself:

> I preach self-will, not revolution. How could I want a revolution? Revolution is war; like all other war, it is a "prolongation of politics by other means." But a man who has once felt the courage to be himself, who has heard the voice of his own destiny, cares nothing for politics, whether it be monarchist or democratic, revolutionary or conservative! He is concerned with something else. His self-will, like the profound, magnificent, God-given self-will that inhabits

197

every blade of grass, has no other aim than his own growth. "Egoism," if you will. But very different from the sordid egoism of those who lust for money or power! . . . Those who distrust the life-giving force within them, or who have none, are driven to compensate through such substitutes as money.[3]

Knecht respects Plinio Designori. But Dasa ultimately must turn to the yogi.

FOOTNOTES

PREFACE:

[1]Joseph Mileck, *Hermann Hesse and His Critics* (Chapel Hill: U. of North Carolina Press, 1958), p. 199.
[2]Hermann Hesse, *Demian* (New York: Bantam, 1966), p. 4.

CHAPTER ONE: *Siddhartha.*

[1] Due to its popularity and wide circulation as well as to a sentimental attachment to this important edition, I will cite the pages of the New Directions text of *Siddhartha* (New York, 1957), rather than using the more recent, less expensive Bantam paperback.

[2]Anyone familiar with the work of Alan W. Watts, especially his fine *Psychotherapy East & West* (New York: Pantheon, 1961), will recognize how much I owe him.

[3]Quoted in Bernhard Zeller, *Portrait of Hesse* (New York: Herder and Herder, 1971), p. 102.

[4]Even to a person who doesn't read German, the opening sentence of *Siddhartha* must suggest the repetitive, almost incantatory quality to which I am referring: *Im Schatten des Hauses, in der Sonne des Flussufers bei den Booten, im Schatten des Salwaldes im Schatten des Feigenbaumes wuchs Siddhartha auf, der schone Sohn des Brahmanen, der junge Falke, zusammen mit Govinda, seinem Freunde, dem Brahmanensohn.* The

German, by the way, is easy enough for a second-semester college student to manage.

[5]Hesse engages in deliberate ambiguity with the word *Atman*. Sometimes he uses it to mean "self" and sometimes to mean "Brahma." Had he wanted to avoid ambiguity in the latter case, he could have accurately referred to *Atman* as *Paramatman*. In German, the word *Atman* permeates the novel, for *atmen* (to breathe) and *Atem* (breath) are used frequently in connection with Siddhartha's meditation techniques.

[6]The sources most useful to me in this section have been the revised edition of John B. Noss' *Man's Religions* (New York: MacMillan, 1956), T. C. Dunham and A. S. Wensinger's fine glossary to the German school edition of *Siddhartha* (New York: MacMillan, 1962), and my association with SIMS—*Jai Guru Dev*.

[7]Hermann Hesse, *Steppenwolf* (New York: Holt, Rinehart, and Winston, 1963), p. 57.

[8]There is a very useful discussion of this point in Theodore Ziolkowski's *The Novels of Hermann Hesse* (Princeton: Princeton U. Press, 1965), pp. 160-70.

[9]Mark Boulby, *Herman Hesse: His Mind and Art* (Ithaca: Cornell U. Press, 1967), p. 142n. *Kamaswami*, however, Boulby translates as "master of the material world" (p. 144n.).

[10]Dunham and Wensinger, pp. 181-2.

[11]I cherish privately the unverified suspicion that Hesse might have experienced a similar trauma in the recent break-up of his family. The episode rings too true; I have seen the powerful anguish of men who have not loved their wives falling tragically in love with their maturing, and departing, sons.

CHAPTER TWO: *Steppenwolf.*

[1]Hermann Hesse, *Steppenwolf* (New York: Holt, Rinehart, and Winston, 1963). This paperback has an excellent brief introduction to Hesse's writings.

[2]The briefest and clearest explanation of the principles of ego, anima, and Self appears in M. L. Franz's "The Process of Individuation," in Carl G. Jung, ed., *Man and His Symbols* (New York: Aldus Books, 1964), pp. 157-224. This whole book is very useful for both *Steppenwolf* and *Narcissus and Goldmund.*

[3]Bernhard Zeller, *Portrait of Hesse,* pp. 105-6.

[4]Joseph Mileck, *Hermann Hesse and His Critics,* p. 25.

[5]Zeller, pp. 114-15.

[6]In *A Dictionary of Symbols* (New York: Philosophical Library, 1962), J. E. Cirlot defines the scorpion: "It corresponds to that period of the span of man's life which lies under the threat of death (that is, the 'fall'). It is also related with the sexual function" (pp. 267-8). This fine reference book is not only useful for Jungians but also for those interested in astrology, colorology, numerology, Tarot, and a wide variety of other Western and Eastern symbolic systems.

[7]Timothy Leary believes that Hesse may have used mescaline; The Magic Theater and Govinda's vision of Siddhartha both point that way. His essay on Hesse, "Poet of the Interior Journey," in *Politics of Ecstasy* (London: MacGibbon and Kee, 1970), is well worth reading. Leary presents some remarkable insights into the major novels, and he does so with brevity and clarity.

[8]Cirlot, p. 131.

[9]Alan Watts, *Psychotherapy East & West,* p. 59.

CHAPTER THREE: *Narcissus and Goldmund.*

[1]Hermann Hesse, *Narcissus and Goldmund* (New York: Farrar, Straus, and Giroux, 1968).

[2]Bernhard Zeller, *Portrait of Hesse,* p. 116.

[3]For the passage on the mother-world, I have drawn on several definitions in J. E. Cirlot's *Dictionary of Symbols,* largely those listed in the index under the headings, "Great Mother" and "Terrible Mother." I am also indirectly indebted to Erich Neumann's *The Great Mother* (New York: Pantheon, 1955), an exhaustive study of the subject.

[4]Zeller, p. 43.

[5]Cirlot, p. 70.

[6]*Ibid.,* p. 108.

[7]Denis deRougemont, *Love in the Western World* (revised edition: New York: Pantheon, 1956). See also Leslie Fiedler's excellent *Love and Death in the American Novel* (revised edition: New York: Dell, 1966).

CHAPTER FOUR: *Magister Ludi.*

[1]Hermann Hesse, *Magister Ludi (The Glass Bead Game)* (New York: Holt, Rinehart, and Winston, 1969). In my opinion, this is the best American edition of *Magister Ludi* available. The translation by Clara and Richard Winston is very good, and the preface by Theodore Ziolkowski is excellent. As Ziolkowski points out, Hesse's title for the novel was *The Glass Bead Game,* and so is the Winstons'. The recent Bantam paperback reinstated the old title. The point is of some significance: it brings into focus an argument over whether the novel is about the Game or about Knecht. I believe they are one and the same. I settle for *Magister Ludi* as title for familiarity and for brevity.

[2]Mark Boulby estimates the date *(Hermann Hesse,* p. 268).

[3]As usual, Hesse's fantasies have a basis in reality. Around the same time that Hesse was completing *Magister Ludi,* Susan K. Langer was investigating the possibilities of synthesizing the arts and sciences through a symbolic system, in her influential book, *Philosophy in a New Key* (Cambridge: Harvard U. Press, 1942).

[4]This League's career is presented in Hesse's fascinating novella, *The Journey to the East* (New York: Farrar, Straus, and Giroux, 1956). This seems to be Timothy Leary's favorite among Hesse's books; see "Poet of the Interior Journey," in *Politics of Ecstasy.*

[5]Carl G. Jung, *Psychology and Religion: West and East* (New York: Pantheon, 1958), p. 604. Jung's article was originally published as the preface to an English edition of the German translation of the *I Ching* that Hesse probably used.

[6]Paraphrased by Paul Oskar Kristeller, *Renaissance Thought* (New York: Harper and Row, 1961), p. 90.

[7]Boulby, p. 302.

[8]Quoted in *ibid.,* p. 303.

[9]J. E. Cirlot, *A Dictionary of Symbols,* p. 210. See also J. C. Middleton, "An Enigma Transfigured," *German Life and Letters,* New Series, X (1956-7), 298-302.

[10]I should point out that Hesse wrote the *Lives* in the early stages of *Magister Ludi* and that some critics believe that there are significant inconsistencies in the novel, which took him twelve years to write. While I will grant that there may be some flaws in *Magister Ludi,* I am not so concerned about Hesse's brick-laying ability as I am about what he was building; the completed edifice, in my view, stands magnificently.

CONCLUSION.

[1]T. S. Eliot, "Tradition and the Individual Talent," in *The Sacred Wood* (New York: Barnes and Noble, 1960), p. 54.

[2]Massimo Teodori, *The New Left* (Indianapolis: Bobbs-Merrill, 1969), p. 36.

[3]Hermann Hesse, *If the War Goes on* . . . (New York: Farrar, Straus, and Giroux, 1971), p. 83.

BIBLIOGRAPHY

Here are the editions of books by Hermann Hesse that I have cited in my text. Each of these books is currently available in at least one American paperback edition.

Demian: The Story of Emil Sinclair's Youth. Translated by Michael Roloff and Michael Lebeck. New York: Bantam, 1966. This edition includes an introduction by Thomas Mann.

If the War Goes On . . . : Reflections on War and Politics. Translated by Ralph Manheim. New York: Farrar, Straus, and Giroux, Inc., 1971. (Noonday paperback.)

The Journey to the East. Translated by Hilda Rosner. New York: Farrar, Straus, and Giroux, Inc., 1956. (Noonday paperback.)

Magister Ludi (The Glass Bead Game). Translated by Richard and Clara Winston. New York: Bantam, 1970. This edition has a very good introduction by Theodore Ziolkowski.

Narcissus and Goldmund. Translated by Ursule Molinaro. New York: Farrar, Straus, and Giroux, 1968.

Siddhartha. Translated by Hilda Rosner. New York: New Directions, 1951.

Steppenwolf. Translated by Basil Creighton; revised by Joseph Mileck and Horst Frenz. New York: Holt, Rinehart, and Winston, 1963. This edition contains a useful introduction and bibliography by Mileck.

These are the books on Hesse that I found most useful:

Boulby, Mark. *Hermann Hesse: His Mind and Art*. Ithaca: Cornell U. Press, 1967.

Mileck, Joseph. *Hermann Hesse and His Critics*. Chapel Hill: U. of North Carolina Press, 1958.

Zeller, Bernhard. *Portrait of Hesse: An Illustrated Biography*, translated by Mark Hollebone. New York: Herder and Herder, 1971.

Ziolkowski, Theodore. *The Novels of Hermann Hesse: A Study in Theme and Structure*. Princeton: Princeton U. Press, 1965.

The following books, though not specifically concerned with Hesse, are illuminating for anyone concerned with his work:

Cirlot, J. E. *A Dictionary of Symbols*, translated by Jack Sage. New York: Philosophical Library, 1962.

Jung, Carl G. *Psychology and Religion: West and East*, translated by R. F. C. Hull. Bolligen Series, XX. New York: Pantheon Books, Inc., 1958.

————, ed. *Man and His Symbols*. London: Aldus Books, Ltd., 1964.

Leary, Timothy. *Politics of Ecstasy*. London: MacGibbon & Kee, Ltd., 1970.

Watts, Alan W. *Psychotherapy East & West*. New York: Pantheon Books, Inc., 1961.